Ninja Creami
Recipe Book with Color Pictures

Effortless & Creative Ninja Foodi Creami Recipes Are Perfect for Crafting Delicious Ice Creams and Delightful Frozen Treats that Everyone Will Adore

Allison Jimmerson

© Copyright 2024
- All Rights Reserved

This document is geared towards providing exact and reliable information with regards to the topic and issue covered. The publication is sold with the idea that the publisher is not required to render accounting, officially permitted, or otherwise, qualified services. If advice is necessary, legal, or professional, a practiced individual in the profession should be ordered. -From a Declaration of Principles which was accepted and approved equally by a Committee of the American Bar Association and a Committee of Publishers and Associations. In no way is it legal to reproduce, duplicate, or transmit any part of this document in either electronic means or in printed format. Recording of this publication is strictly prohibited and any storage of this document is not allowed unless with written permission from the publisher.

All rights reserved. The information provided herein is stated to be truthful and consistent, in that any liability, in terms of inattention or otherwise, by any usage or abuse of any policies, processes, or directions contained within is the solitary and utter responsibility of the recipient reader.

Under no circumstances will any legal responsibility or blame be held against the publisher for any reparation, damages, or monetary loss due to the information herein, either directly or indirectly. Respective authors own all copyrights not held by the publisher.

The information herein is offered for informational purposes solely, and is universal as so. The presentation of the information is without contract or any type of guarantee assurance. The trademarks that are used are without any consent, and the publication of the trademark is without permission or backing by the trademark owner.

All trademarks and brands within this book are for clarifying purposes only and are the owned by the owners themselves, not affiliated with this document.

>> CONTENTS

- ❖ 01   Introduction
- ❖ 02   Fundamentals of Ninja Creami
- ❖ 10   Chapter 1 Sorbet
- ❖ 19   Chapter 2 Smoothie Bowls
- ❖ 28   Chapter 3 Milkshake
- ❖ 37   Chapter 4 Ice Creams
- ❖ 45   Chapter 5 Ice Cream Mix-In
- ❖ 53   Chapter 6 Gelato
- ❖ 66   Conclusion
- ❖ 67   Appendix 1 Measurement Conversion Chart
- ❖ 68   Appendix 2 Recipes Index

Introduction

Yummy frozen treats in minutes! That's what this Ninja Creami cookbook promises. Open it up to find delicious recipes for ice creams, gelatos, sorbets, smoothies, and more cold delights. These treats taste like they came from your favorite ice cream shop, but you make them right at home.

The Ninja Creami is a handy kitchen gadget that whips up creamy frozen desserts with the touch of a button. Just choose a recipe, freeze the ingredients in the freezer-safe Ninja pint, and let the machine work magic. In minutes, you'll have everything from strawberry ice cream to blueberry milkshake ready to enjoy. No complicated steps or special skills are required.

New to making frozen treats? No problem! The cookbook starts with tips to get you going. Learn how to swap ingredients to make recipes dairy-free or low-sugar. Discover quick "no-prep" ideas that use items already in your fridge and pantry. Let your creativity run wild by mixing and matching flavors. With so many options, every treat can be personalized.

The Ninja Creami cookbook makes it a breeze to create gourmet frozen desserts at home. Impress your family and friends with your icy creations. Stay cool and satisfied all summer long! Treat yourself to homemade ice cream and more - the Ninja Creami way.

Fundamentals of Ninja Creami

What is Ninja Creami?

Are you yearning for some chilly sweetness? Well, let's introduce you to the Ninja Creami! This kitchen appliance is your ticket to crafting homemade frozen delights like ice cream, smoothie, sorbet, and milkshakes – and it's really easy to use.

Picture this: a sleek, compact design that fits perfectly on your countertop. The heart of this dessert maker resides in the base, where a sturdy motor does all the heavy lifting. At the top, you'll find a digital display and a dial, essential for choosing preset programs to create frozen treats. And, of course, there's the power button to start and stop your dessert adventure.

Here's where the magic happens: inside the plastic outer bowl. It's like a protective nest for a freezer-safe Ninja Creami pint, where you'll stash all your yummy ingredients. Perched on top of this outer bowl, there's the Creamerizer paddle, an attachment ready to make dessert dreams come true. As the Creami pint twirls, the paddle blends and churns your mixture into creamy perfection.

So, let's dive into the process. First, you'll prepare your base ingredients and put them into one of the Creami pints. The real enchantment takes place overnight in the freezer, turning your mix into a frosty canvas ready for creativity. Once your frozen masterpiece sits comfortably in the outer bowl, it's time to pick your program.

Are you in the mood for ice cream or maybe a fruity sorbet? No problem – the Creami's got your back. The Creamerizer paddle gets to work, blending, churning, and aerating your concoction into that perfect, velvety texture you've been dreaming of. And here's the best part – you can toss in extra flavors and mix-ins, adding your unique touch to every spoonful.

What truly sets the Ninja Creami apart is its simplicity. No more worrying about consistency or timing like with old-school ice cream makers. This clever machine does all the hard work, automatically stopping when your dessert reaches perfection.

Now, let's talk about cleanup. After indulging in your delightful dessert, the last thing you want is a pile of dishes. But fear not, because the Creami's got your back. Every part can be easily cleaned, from the Creami pints to the lids and even the trusty Creamerizer paddle. Whether you prefer doing it by hand or letting the dishwasher handle it, the Creami is a breeze to maintain.

In a nutshell, the Ninja Creami is your one-stop solution for whipping up frozen dessert magic right in your own kitchen. It's a brilliant blend of clever design and preset programs, making homemade ice cream a reality for beginners and seasoned dessert aficionados. So, prepare to embark on a delightful dessert journey with your new kitchen superstar – the Ninja Creami!

Benefits of Using Ninja Creami

Welcome to the world of Ninja Creami, where you can turn your frozen dessert dreams into reality. This innovative kitchen appliance brings a world of delightful frozen treats to your home. Now, let's explore the fantastic benefits of owning this versatile device.

1. Creative Culinary Playground:
Ninja Creami isn't just an appliance; it's your gateway to culinary creativity. Imagine crafting your own personalized ice cream flavors, experimenting with unique combinations of mix-ins, or transforming seasonal fruits into refreshing sorbets. With this versatile machine, you become the master of flavor, texture, and presentation.

2. Wholesome Ingredients, Complete Control:
When you create frozen treats at home, you're in charge of the ingredients. You can opt for fresh, organic fruits, high-quality dairy or dairy-free alternatives, and natural sweeteners. Say goodbye to artificial additives and excess sugars found in store-bought desserts. Ninja Creami lets you indulge without compromising your dietary preferences.

3. Quick and Effortless Magic:
Gone are the days of laborious churning and monitoring. Ninja Creami does the heavy lifting for you. With its preset programs, crafting frozen treats becomes as easy as selecting your desired program and letting the machine work magic. You'll have velvety ice cream or luscious yogurt ready to savor in minutes.

4. Tailored Treats for All Tastes:
Whether you're a die-hard chocoholic, a fruit fanatic, or a nutty aficionado, Ninja Creami has a treat for you. The customizable nature of your creations ensures that everyone's cravings are satisfied. Get inventive by infusing your bases with extracts, spices, or even a hint of espresso for that extra kick.

5. Family Bonding and Entertainment:
Making frozen treats with Ninja Creami is a beautiful way to bond with your loved ones. Gather around as you pour ingredients into the Creami pints, select programs, and eagerly anticipate the delightful outcome. It's an activity that brings joy to all ages and adds excitement to your daily routine.

6. Healthier Indulgence:
Indulgence doesn't have to equate to guilt. Ninja Creami allows you to indulge in frozen desserts without compromising your health goals. Control over ingredients means you can choose alternatives that align with dietary restrictions, ensuring that you enjoy your treats guilt-free.

7. Limitless Flavor Adventures:
With Ninja Creami, you're not limited to store shelves' offerings. Unleash your imagination and embark on flavor adventures that you never thought possible. From classic vanilla to exotic mango chili, there's no boundary to the taste sensations you can create.

8. Economical Delights:
Regular trips to ice cream parlors can add up quickly. With Ninja Creami, you're investing in a one-time purchase that yields endless batches of frozen perfection. You'll save money over time while treating yourself to premium-quality treats.

9. Show-Stopping Desserts:
Impress your guests and elevate your dessert game with artisanal creations. From elegant dinner parties to casual gatherings, Ninja Creami lets you showcase your culinary prowess and leave a lasting impression on your guests.

10. Ongoing Inspiration:
The journey with Ninja Creami is a never-ending source of inspiration. As you explore recipes, try new techniques, and experiment with ingredients, you'll find that the possibilities are boundless. It's a kitchen companion that keeps on giving.

11. Say Farewell to Preservatives:
Commercially-made frozen desserts often come loaded with preservatives to extend their shelf life. Ninja Creami lets you skip these additives entirely. Your homemade treats are as fresh as can be, free from unwanted chemicals.

12. Temperature Control Matters:
Precise temperature control is the secret sauce behind perfect frozen treats. Ninja Creami's technology ensures that your desserts are churned and frozen at the ideal temperature. The result? Creamy, dreamy delights every time.

13. Versatile Serving Options:
The Ninja Creami offers versatile serving options, allowing you to create a variety of frozen delights such as creamy ice cream, refreshing sorbet, indulgent gelato, and nutritious smoothie bowls. This multifunctionality makes it an ideal addition to any kitchen, catering to diverse tastes and dietary preferences effortlessly.

Fundamentals of Ninja Creami

14. Wholesome for the Whole Family:
Whether you're a parent serving up nutritious yogurt for your kids or a health-conscious individual keeping track of calories, Ninja Creami caters to all. It's your tool for crafting treats that align with your family's dietary needs.

15. Perfect Portions, Less Waste:
Serving size matters, and Ninja Creami helps you keep it in check. The Creami pints are the perfect vessel for single servings or intimate gatherings. This means less waste and more enjoyment.

16. The Joy of Seasonal Sensations:
Make the most of seasonal fruits and flavors with Ninja Creami. As the seasons change, so can your creations. Summer strawberries, autumnal apples, or winter spices—all can be transformed into delightful frozen confections.

17. Allergy-Friendly Alternatives:
Food allergies or sensitivities need not keep you from enjoying frozen treats. Ninja Creami lets you choose allergen-free ingredients, such as nut milk, soy yogurt, or gluten-free cookies, so everyone can indulge together.

18. Stress-Free cleanup:
After the indulgence comes the cleanup. Thankfully, Ninja Creami keeps this task hassle-free. The Creami pints, lids, and Creamerizer paddle are dishwasher-safe, making cleanup a breeze.

19. Recipe Expansion:
As you become more familiar with your Ninja Creami, you'll discover countless recipes to try. Explore the world of ice cream, sorbet, gelato, and even dairy-free alternatives like coconut-based ice cream. Your culinary repertoire will expand beyond imagination.

20. Unforgettable Family Traditions:
Start a new tradition with Ninja Creami. Whether it's a weekly sundae night, a birthday ice cream cake, or a spontaneous treat day, your family will cherish these moments created with love and a touch of homemade magic.

There you have it, a comprehensive look at the benefits of using Ninja Creami. From creative freedom and healthier choices to unforgettable family moments, this remarkable appliance transforms your kitchen into a frozen dessert paradise. With Ninja Creami, the joy of crafting and indulging in frozen delights knows no bounds.

Step-By-Step Using the Ninja Creami

Welcome to the hands-on part of the Ninja Creami journey. In this section, we'll go through the process step by step, ensuring you have everything you need to create your frozen masterpieces. There is no magic, no mysteries, just a clear path to creamy success.

Step 1: Unbox and Assemble
When you first lay eyes on your Ninja Creami, the excitement might be overwhelming. Take a breath; we're here to guide you. Begin by unboxing your Ninja Creami. Inside, you'll find essential components:

- **Base Unit:** This is the heart of your Creami. It houses the motor and all the smarts that make your frozen dreams come true. Find a sturdy, flat spot on your countertop, and place it there.

- **Outer Bowl:** This is where the action happens. It holds the Creami pint with your ingredients. Place it securely onto the base unit.
- **Creamerizer Paddle:** This paddle is the key to achieving that creamy, dreamy texture. Insert it into the outer bowl's lid.
- **Creami Pint:** You'll receive a set of BPA-free Pints. These are your canvases for creating frozen delights.

Step 2: Plug In and Power Up

Safety first! Before diving in, ensure the Creami is unplugged. Then, connect it to a power source. It's essential to plug in your Creami before attaching the outer bowl. This simple step ensures everything runs smoothly.

Step 3: Create Your Base

Here's where your culinary creativity shines. You can make ice cream, smoothie, sorbet, or any other frosty treat your heart desires. The key is to prepare your base mix, pour it into a Creami Pint, and let it chill in the freezer for a few hours or overnight. This step is like laying the foundation for your frozen masterpiece.

Step 4: Assemble for Churning

Once your base is thoroughly chilled, take the outer bowl and insert your frozen Creami Pint into it. Be sure everything is lined up securely so you're ready for the next step.

Step 5: Pick Your Program

Now, here's where the fun begins. The Creami offers various preset programs for different treats. Select your desired program: Ice Cream, Sorbet, Lite Ice Cream, Smoothie Bowl, Gelato, Milkshake and Mix-In. Each program is designed for specific freezing zones within the pint.

Step 6: Start Churning

With your program selected, it's time to start the Creami. Press the power button, and your Creami will begin churning. Watch in awe as the Creamerizer paddle spins, working its magic on your base mixture. You do no need to babysit; the Creami will stop when your treat is perfectly churned.

Step 7: Add Mix-Ins (If Desired)

This step is where you can get extra creative. If you want to add mix-ins like nuts, chocolate chips, or fruit, there's a specific program for that, too. Follow the instructions in the manual to add your mix-ins and let the Creami do the work.

Step 8: Serve and Enjoy

Once your Creami completes its program, you can scoop out your frozen masterpiece. Grab your favorite bowl or cone, and savor the fruits of your labor. Deliciousness awaits!

Step 9: Shutdown and Disassembly

Let's ensure your Creami is safe to handle. First, turn off the power using the power button. Then, unplug the unit from the power source. Safety is paramount.

With the Creami powered down, it's time to disassemble the parts. Start by unlocking the lid of the outer bowl by twisting it counterclockwise. Then, remove the outer bowl from the base unit by turning the handle counterclockwise as well. Now, it's safe to remove the Creami Pint and the Creamerizer paddle from the outer bowl.

And there you have it—a complete guide to using and maintaining your Ninja Creami. With these steps in your repertoire, you're well-prepared to embark on a delicious journey into the world of homemade frozen treats. From ice cream to sorbet and everything in between, your Ninja Creami is your ticket to frozen dessert bliss.

You're ready to impress friends and family with your culinary prowess. Treat them to an array of frozen delights and bask in the joy of creating sweet memories together.

Tips for Using Accessories

Let's delve into some valuable tips for harnessing the full potential of your Ninja Creami accessories. These pointers will elevate your frozen creations to a whole new level.

1. Creative Mix-Ins
Experiment with various mix-ins to create unique flavors and textures. Think chocolate chips, crushed cookies, fruit chunks, or even a swirl of caramel. The possibilities are endless, so don't be afraid to get creative.

2. Perfectly Pre-Chilled Pints
Ensure your Creami Pints are thoroughly chilled before use for the creamiest results. Pop them in the freezer for a few hours or, better yet, overnight. This helps maintain the ideal temperature for the Creamerizer paddle to work its magic.

3. Patience Is a Virtue
Once your Creami program is complete, resist the urge to dig in immediately. Let your frozen masterpiece sit in the Creami Pint for a minute or two. This brief waiting period lets it firm slightly, resulting in a smoother, more enjoyable texture.

4. Optimal Pour-Ins
When adding pour-ins like flavored syrups or liquors, be mindful of quantity. Too much liquid can affect the final consistency of your frozen treat. Follow the recommended measurements in your recipes for the best results.

5. Keep It Simple
While it's fun to experiment, simplicity can often lead to outstanding results. Classic flavors like vanilla or chocolate can be just as satisfying as intricate creations. Sometimes, less is more.

6. Cleaning Hacks
To make cleaning even easier, rinse the Creamerizer paddle and Creami Pint immediately after use. This prevents stubborn residue from drying and sticking to the parts, making cleanup a breeze.

7. Double Trouble
Why make one flavor when you can make two? Utilize your Creami's capabilities to craft dual-flavor delights. The user guide provides tips on creating two flavors from a single base, doubling the joy.

8. Frozen Fruit Fun
Combine frozen fruits like berries, mangoes, or peaches for a refreshing twist. These fruits add a burst of flavor and contribute to a healthier treat.

9. Temperature Matters
Pay attention to the temperature of your base. If it's too cold and firm, consider using the RE-SPIN function before adding mix-ins. This ensures a smoother blend and avoids overworking the Creamerizer paddle.

These practical tips will help you make the most of your Ninja Creami accessories. Prepare to embark on a delicious journey, exploring new flavors and enjoying the creamy wonders this kitchen companion offers.

Cleaning and Caring for Ninja Creami

Properly caring for your Ninja Creami is essential to ensure it continues to serve up those delightful frozen creations. Let's get into the nitty-gritty of cleaning and maintaining this fantastic kitchen companion.

Shutdown and Disassembly

Before diving into the cleaning process, take a moment to ensure your Creami is safe to handle. Begin by turning off the power using the power button. After that, unplug the unit from the power source. Safety always comes first.

With the Creami powered down, it's time to disassemble the parts. Begin by unlocking the lid of the outer bowl. Give it a counterclockwise twist to release it. Now, remove the outer bowl from the base unit by turning the handle counterclockwise as well. Once that's done, it's safe to remove the Creami Pint and the Creamerizer paddle from the outer bowl.

Cleaning the Parts

The good news is that your Ninja Creami parts are dishwasher-safe, making cleanup a breeze. Place the Creami Pint, lid, and Creamerizer paddle on the top rack of your dishwasher. Let the machine do its thing; your parts will come out clean and ready for action.

However, if you prefer to wash things by hand, that's fine too. Use a mild dish detergent and warm water to clean the Creami Pint, lid, and paddle. Give them a good rinse and allow them to air dry.

Wipe Down the Base

While the main components are in the dishwasher or drying, take a moment to give the base unit some attention. Use a damp cloth to wipe down the exterior of the base unit, ensuring it's free from spills or splatters. Before you plug it in for your next Creami adventure, ensure the unit is completely dry.

Storage

When your Creami is not in use, it's a good idea to store it properly. The Creami Pints and lids can be stacked neatly, and the Creamerizer paddle can be stored separately. Ensure all parts are dry before storing them to prevent unwanted odors or mold growth.

Troubleshooting

If you ever encounter issues with your Ninja Creami, don't worry. The user guide provides a helpful troubleshooting section to address common concerns. Whether it's an issue with the power, assembly, or performance, you'll find valuable tips to help you get things back on track.

So there you have it—a complete guide to cleaning and caring for your Ninja Creami. With these steps, you'll keep your Creami in excellent shape, ready to whip up frozen delights whenever the craving strikes.

Frequently Asked Questions & Notes

Let's address some common questions and important notes about your Ninja Creami. These insights will help you become a true Creami maestro.

FAQs

1. What is the difference between the Creami Pints and regular ice cream containers?

Creami Pints are specially designed for the Creami, ensuring optimal freezing and blending for perfect consistency.

2. Can I use my own containers with the Creami?
For the best results, it's recommended to stick with the Creami Pints provided. They are designed to work seamlessly with the Creami.

3. How long should I freeze the Creami Pints before use?
Overnight freezing is ideal for achieving the creamiest results. A minimum of 8 hours is recommended.

4. What is the RE-SPIN function for?
RE-SPIN is used to further blend and smoothen your dessert, especially if you've added mix-ins or your base is cold.

5. Is the Creami suitable for lactose-free or dairy-free recipes?
Absolutely! You can substitute dairy with alternatives like almond, coconut, or soy milk for equally delicious results.

6. Can I make gelato with the Creami?
Yes, you can! The Creami offers a gelato program that churns your mixture to the perfect gelato consistency.

7. What should I do if the Creami doesn't start when I press the dial?
Ensure the outer bowl is securely placed on the base, and check that the unit is plugged in correctly.

8. Can I make frozen yogurt with probiotics?
Definitely! You can add probiotics to your yogurt base and churn it with the Creami to enjoy frozen yogurt with health benefits.

9. Can I use frozen fruit in my recipes, or should it be fresh?
Frozen fruit works perfectly and adds a delightful chill to your creations. There's no need to thaw it beforehand.

10. Can I make dairy-free sorbets with the Creami?
Absolutely! The Creami is versatile enough to craft dairy-free sorbets using fruit puree, sugar, and a touch of lemon juice.

11. What do I do if my frozen dessert turns out too soft?
Place it in the freezer for a short while to firm up. The Creami creates a soft-serve consistency, which can be hardened in the freezer.

12. Can I make dairy-free ice cream that's just as creamy as traditional ice cream?
Absolutely! Using ingredients like coconut milk or cashew cream can produce dairy-free ice cream with a rich and creamy texture.

13: How do I make sure my frozen dessert is safe to eat, especially if I'm using raw eggs in my recipe?
If your recipe includes raw eggs, consider using pasteurized eggs to reduce the risk. Alternatively, explore eggless recipes for peace of mind.

14. Can I prepare multiple batches of frozen desserts in one

Fundamentals of Ninja Creami

go with the Creami?

Certainly! If you have extra Creami Pints, you can make multiple batches consecutively.

Notes

1. Safety First:
Always read and follow the safety instructions provided in the manual before using your Creami.

2. Program Variations:
Depending on your Creami model, the number of Creami Pints and the available programs may vary. Refer to your specific model's manual for details.

3. Texture Adjustments:
If your frozen dessert isn't as firm as you'd like, transfer it to an airtight container and place it in the freezer for a few hours.

4. Mix-In Timing:
Remember to add mix-ins during the MIX-IN program and not before. This ensures even distribution and perfect incorporation.

5. Freeze Your Pints:
Always ensure your Creami Pints are properly frozen before use. A dedicated freezer shelf can help maintain consistent temperatures.

6. Texture Adjustments
Experiment with different sweeteners and thickeners to achieve the exact texture you desire.

7. Unique Toppings:
Elevate your frozen desserts with inventive toppings like candied nuts, fruit compotes, or flavored syrups.

8. Prepare Mix-Ins in Advance:
If you plan to add mix-ins, prepare them beforehand to streamline the process.

9. Texture Troubleshooting:
If your dessert isn't as creamy as you'd like, try adjusting the fat content or adding stabilizers like guar gum or xanthan gum.

10. Experiment Freely:
Don't hesitate to tweak recipes or invent your own. The Creami is all about exploring new flavors and textures.

With these FAQs and additional notes, you're well-equipped to embark on a delightful journey with your Ninja Creami. Enjoy crafting a wide range of frozen desserts and experimenting with various flavors, textures, and ingredients.

Chapter 1 Sorbet

Pineapple and Mango Sorbet 11

Orange Sorbet 11

Lime Apple Pie Sorbet 12

Peach Sorbet 12

Persimmon Sorbet with Condensed Milk 13

Cherry Pomegranate Sorbet 13

Lemon Sorbet 14

Lemony Coconut Mango Sorbet 14

Plum Sorbet 15

Lime Mango Sorbet 15

Sweet Apricot Sorbet 16

Banana Sorbet 16

Lemon Blueberry Sorbet 17

Pear Sorbet 17

Refreshing Lemon Herb Sorbet 18

Gooseberry Sorbet 18

Pineapple and Mango Sorbet

⏱ **Prep: 5 minutes** ❖ **Serves: 2**

Ingredients:

¾ cup ripe pineapple, cut into ½-inch pieces
1 ripe banana, cut into ½-inch slices
1¼ mangoes, peeled, cut into ½-inch pieces

Preparation:

1. In a Ninja CREAMi pint, move the mangoes along with the pineapples and bananas, and fasten the container with a lid. 2. Freeze the pint for 24 hours. 3. After 24 hours, open the pint, fix it into the outer bowl of Ninja CREAMi, along with the 'Creamerizer paddle'. 4. Fasten the lid, turn on the unit, and select the 'SORBET' function. 5. Dish out the sorbet from the pint and serve chilled.

Serving Suggestions: Top with mango slices and mint leaves.
Variation Tip: You can add some sugar for enhanced sweetness.
Nutritional Information per Serving:
Calories: 203 | Fat: 0.6g | Sat Fat: 0.2g | Carbohydrates: 52g | Fiber: 7.6g | Sugar: 34g | Protein: 3g

Orange Sorbet

⏱ **Prep: 10 minutes** ❖ **Servings: 4**

Ingredients:

1 (20-ounce) can mandarin oranges with liquid

Preparation:

1. Place the orange pieces into an empty Ninja CREAMi container to the MAX FILL line. 2. Cover the orange pieces with liquid from the can. 3. Cover the container with storage lid and freeze for 24 hours. 4. After 24 hours, remove the lid from container and arrange into the outer bowl of Ninja CREAMi. 5. Install the "Creamerizer Paddle" onto the lid of outer bowl. 6. Then rotate the lid clockwise to lock. 7. Press "Power" button to turn on the unit. 8. Then press "SORBET" button. 9. When the program is completed, turn the outer bowl and release it from the machine. 10. Transfer the sorbet into serving bowls and enjoy immediately.

Serving Suggestions: Serve with a garnishing of fresh mint.
Variation Tip: Add a splash of vodka.
Nutritional Information per Serving:
Calories: 52 |Fat: 0g|Sat Fat: 0g|Carbohydrates: 13.6g |Fiber: 1g |Sugar: 12.6g |Protein: 0.9g

Chapter 1 Sorbet

Lime Apple Pie Sorbet

Prep: 10 minutes **Serves: 4**

Ingredients:

1 (21-ounce can) apple pie filling
¼ cup fresh lime juice
1 teaspoon lime zest

Preparation:

1. In an empty Ninja CREAMi pint container, place apple pie filling, lime juice and lime zest and stir to blend. 2. Cover the container with storage lid and freeze for 24 hours. 3. After 24 hours, remove the lid from container and arrange into the outer bowl of Ninja CREAMi. 4. Install the "Creamerizer Paddle" onto the lid of outer bowl. 5. Then rotate the lid clockwise to lock. 6. Press "Power" button to turn on the unit. 7. Then press "SORBET" button. 8. When the program is completed, turn the outer bowl and release it from the machine. 9. Transfer the sorbet into serving bowls and enjoy immediately.

Serving Suggestions: Serve with a drizzling of caramel sauce.
Variation Tip: use freshly squeezed lemon juice.
Nutritional Information per Serving:
Calories: 150 |Fat: 0.2g|Sat Fat: 0g|Carbohydrates: 39.1g|Fiber: 1.5g|Sugar: 20.6g|Protein: 0.2g

Peach Sorbet

Prep: 5 minutes **Cook: 5 minutes** **Serves: 1**

Ingredients:

1 canned peaches

Preparation:

1. Pour the canned peaches (with their liquid) into a ninja CREAMi Pint container and freeze on a level surface in a cold freezer for a full 24 hours. 2. After 24 hours, remove the Pint from the freezer. Remove the lid. 3. Place the Ninja CREAMi Pint into the outer bowl. Place the outer bowl with the Pint in it into the ninja CREAMi machine and turn until the outer bowl locks into place. Push the SORBET button. During the SORBET function, the sorbet will mix together and become very creamy. This should take approximately 2 minutes. 4. Once done, turn the outer bowl and release it from the ninja CREAMi machine. 5. Your sorbet is ready to eat! Enjoy!

Serving Suggestion: Serve immediately.
Variation Tip: Add some fresh mint.
Nutritional Information per Serving:
Calories 169 | Protein 4g | Carbohydrate 41g | Dietary Fiber 6g | Sugar 27g | Fat 1g | Sodium 256mg

Persimmon Sorbet with Condensed Milk

⏰ **Prep:** 10 minutes 🍂 **Serves:** 4

Ingredients:
1¾-liter ice cream, softened
2 cups persimmon pulp
½ can condensed milk, sweetened

Preparation:
1. In a bowl, merge the persimmon pulp with condensed milk and ice cream. 2. In a Ninja CREAMi pint, move the mixture and fasten the container with a lid. 3. Freeze the pint for 24 hours. 4. After 24 hours, open the pint, fix it into the outer bowl of Ninja CREAMi along with the 'Creamerizer paddle'. 5. Fasten the lid, turn on the 'Power Button', and select the 'SORBET' function. 6. Dish out the sorbet from the pint and serve chilled.

Serving Suggestions: Top with condensed milk.
Variation Tip: You can also serve with whipped topping.
Nutritional Information per Serving:
Calories: 183 | Fat: 6g | Sat Fat: 4g | Carbohydrates: 27g | Fiber: 0.2g | Sugar: 26g | Protein: 4g

Cherry Pomegranate Sorbet

⏰ **Prep:** 15 minutes 🍂 **Serves:** 3

Ingredients:
½ cup pomegranate juice
1 can cherries

Preparation:
1. In a Ninja CREAMi pint, move the cherries and juice and fasten the container with a lid. 2. Freeze the pint for 24 hours. 3. After 24 hours, open the pint, fix it into the outer bowl of Ninja CREAMi, along with the 'Creamerizer paddle.' 4. Fasten the lid, turn on the unit, and select the 'SORBET' function. 5. Dish out the sorbet from the pint and serve chilled.

Serving Suggestions: Top with pomegranate arils.
Variation Tip: You can add maple syrup for more taste.
Nutritional Information per Serving:
Calories: 110 | Fat: 0.5g | Sat Fat: 0g | Carbohydrates: 28g | Fiber: 2.8g | Sugar: 23g | Protein: 1.2g

Lemon Sorbet

⏱ Prep: 10 minutes   🍽 Serves: 4

Ingredients:

1 cup warm water
½ cup fresh lemon juice
¼ cup trehalose sugar
1 tablespoon agave nectar

Preparation:

1. In a large-sized bowl, add water and remaining ingredients and whisk until blended thoroughly. 2. Transfer the blended mixture into an empty Ninja CREAMi pint container. 3. Cover the container with storage lid and freeze for 24 hours. 4. After 24 hours, remove the lid from container and arrange into the outer bowl of Ninja CREAMi. 5. Install the "Creamerizer Paddle" onto the lid of outer bowl. 6. Then rotate the lid clockwise to lock. 7. Press "Power" button to turn on the unit. 8. Then press "SORBET" button. 9. When the program is completed, turn the outer bowl and release it from the machine. 10. Transfer the sorbet into serving bowls and enjoy immediately.

Serving Suggestions: Serve with a garnishing of lemon peel.
Variation Tip: You can substitute trehalose sugar with ½ cup of white sugar.
Nutritional Information per Serving:
Calories: 69 |Fat: 0.2g|Sat Fat: 0.2g|Carbohydrates: 17.1g|Fiber: 0.4g|Sugar: 16.9g|Protein: 0.2g

Lemony Coconut Mango Sorbet

⏱ Prep: 10 minutes   🍽 Serves: 6

Ingredients:

3 ripe mangoes, sliced
2 tablespoons lemon juice
1 tablespoon lemon zest
3 cups dairy-free coconut milk ice cream
A few mint leaves

Preparation:

1. Add all the ingredients to a blender. Mix well until smooth. 2. Pour the mixture into the Ninja CREAMi Pint and close the lid. 3. Place the pint into the freezer and freeze for 24 hours. 4. Once done, open the lid and place the pint into the outer bowl of the Ninja CREAMi. Set the Creamerizer Paddle into the outer bowl. 5. Lock the lid by rotating it clockwise. 6. Turn the unit on and press the SORBET button. 7. Once done, take out the bowl from the Ninja CREAMi. 8. Serve and enjoy this yummy sorbet.

Serving Suggestions: Drizzle with coconut or mint leaves.
Variation Tip: Add vanilla essence for a taste variation.
Nutritional Information per Serving:
Calories: 184 | Fat: 4.2g | Sat Fat: 3.2g | Carbohydrates: 39.6g | Fiber: 6.3g | Sugar: 32g | Protein: 1.9g

Plum Sorbet

⏰ **Prep: 10 minutes** 📚 **Serves: 4**

Ingredients:
2 pounds fresh plums, pitted and chopped
2 tablespoons amaretto
2 teaspoons honey

Preparation:
1. In a high-powered blender, add plums, amaretto and honey and process until smooth. 2. Transfer the blended mixture into an empty Ninja CREAMi pint container. 3. Cover the container with storage lid and freeze for 24 hours. 4. After 24 hours, remove the lid from container and arrange into the outer bowl of Ninja CREAMi. 5. Install the "Creamerizer Paddle" onto the lid of outer bowl. 6. Then rotate the lid clockwise to lock. 7. Press "Power" button to turn on the unit. 8. Then press "SORBET" button. 9. When the program is completed, turn the outer bowl and release it from the machine. 10. Transfer the sorbet into serving bowls and enjoy immediately.

Serving Suggestions: Serve with a topping of coconut.
Variation Tip: Chocolate liqueur can be used instead of amaretto.
Nutritional Information per Serving:
Calories: 48 |Fat: 0.1g|Sat Fat: 0g|Carbohydrates: 6.9g|Fiber: 0.5g|Sugar: 12.4g|Protein: 0.3g

Lime Mango Sorbet

⏰ **Prep: 10 minutes** 📚 **Serves: 4**

Ingredients:
3 cups frozen mango chunks
½ cup full-fat coconut milk
2 tablespoons maple syrup
2 tablespoons fresh lime juice
1 teaspoon lime zest
1-2 teaspoons chili lime seasoning

Preparation:
1. In a high-powered blender, add mango chunks and remaining ingredients and process until smooth. 2. Transfer the blended mixture into an empty Ninja CREAMi pint container. 3. Cover the container with storage lid and freeze for 24 hours. 4. After 24 hours, remove the lid from container and arrange into the outer bowl of Ninja CREAMi. 5. Install the "Creamerizer Paddle" onto the lid of outer bowl. 6. Then rotate the lid clockwise to lock. 7. Press "Power" button to turn on the unit. 8. Then press "SORBET" button. 9. When the program is completed, turn the outer bowl and release it from the machine. 10. Transfer the sorbet into serving bowls and enjoy immediately.

Serving Suggestions: Garnish with lime zest before serving.
Variation Tip: Use chili lime seasoning according to your taste.
Nutritional Information per Serving:
Calories: 166 |Fat: 6.5g|Sat Fat: 5.6g|Carbohydrates: 27.4g|Fiber: 2g|Sugar: 23.4g|Protein: 1.5g

Sweet Apricot Sorbet

⏱ **Prep: 40 minutes** ❖ **Serves: 8**

Ingredients:
2 tablespoons lemon juice, freshly squeezed
2 cups apricots, chopped and pitted
1 cup hot water
1 cup sugar, granulated

Preparation:
1. Blitz apricots with all other ingredients in a blender until smooth. 2. In a Ninja CREAMi pint, move the mixture and fasten the container with a lid. 3. Freeze the pint for 24 hours. 4. After 24 hours, open the pint, fix it into the outer bowl of Ninja CREAMi along with the 'Creamerizer paddle'. 5. Fasten the lid, turn on the 'Power Button', and select the 'SORBET' function. 6. Dish out the sorbet from the pint and serve chilled.

Serving Suggestions: Top with the mint leaves.
Variation Tip: You can use honey instead of sugar.
Nutritional Information per Serving:
Calories: 116 | Fat: 1g | Sat Fat: 1g | Carbohydrates: 30g | Fiber: 1g | Sugar: 29g | Protein: 1g

Banana Sorbet

⏱ **Prep: 5 minutes** 🍲 **Cook: 3minutes** ❖ **Serves: 4**

Ingredients:
4 large bananas
Water, as required

Preparation:
1. In a blender, blitz all the ingredients until smooth. 2. In a Ninja CREAMi pint, move the mixture and fasten the container with a lid. 3. Freeze the pint for 24 hours. 4. After 24 hours, open the pint, fix it into the outer bowl of Ninja CREAMi along with the 'Creamerizer paddle'. 5. Fasten the lid, turn on the 'Power Button', and select the 'SORBET' function. 6. Dish out the sorbet from the pint and serve chilled.

Serving Suggestions: Serve topped with banana slices.
Variation Tip: You can add some sugar for enhanced sweetness.
Nutritional Information per Serving:
Calories: 61 | Fat: 0.2g | Sat Fat: 0.1g | Carbohydrates: 15.5g | Fiber: 1.8g | Sugar: 8.3g | Protein: 0.7g

Lemon Blueberry Sorbet

⏲ **Prep: 10 minutes**   ≽ **Serves: 4**

> Ingredients:

4 cups frozen blueberries
½ cup water
3 tablespoons honey
3 tablespoons fresh lemon juice
½ teaspoon lemon zest

> Preparation:

1. In a high-powered blender, add blueberries and remaining ingredients and process until smooth. 2. Transfer the blended mixture into an empty Ninja CREAMi pint container. 3. Cover the container with storage lid and freeze for 24 hours. 4. After 24 hours, remove the lid from container and arrange into the outer bowl of Ninja CREAMi. 5. Install the "Creamerizer Paddle" onto the lid of outer bowl. 6. Then rotate the lid clockwise to lock. 7. Press "Power" button to turn on the unit. 8. Then press "SORBET" button. 9. When the program is completed, turn the outer bowl and release it from the machine. 10. Transfer the sorbet into serving bowls and enjoy immediately.

Serving Suggestions: Serve with a topping of fresh blueberries.
Variation Tip: Strictly follow the ratio of ingredients.
Nutritional Information per Serving:
Calories: 134 |Fat: 0.6g|Sat Fat: 0.1g|Carbohydrates: 34.3g|Fiber: 3.6g|Sugar: 27.6g|Protein: 1.3g

Pear Sorbet

⏲ **Prep: 10 minutes**   ≽ **Serves: 4**

> Ingredients:

1 (15-ounce) can pears in light syrup

> Preparation:

1. Place the pear pieces into an empty Ninja CREAMi container to the MAX FILL line. 2. Cover the pear pieces with syrup from the can. 3. Transfer the blended mixture into an empty Ninja CREAMi pint container. 4. Cover the container with storage lid and freeze for 24 hours. 5. After 24 hours, remove the lid from container and arrange into the outer bowl of Ninja CREAMi. 6. Install the "Creamerizer Paddle" onto the lid of outer bowl. 7. Then rotate the lid clockwise to lock. 8. Press "Power" button to turn on the unit. 9. Then press "SORBET" button. 10. When the program is completed, turn the outer bowl and release it from the machine. 11. Transfer the sorbet into serving bowls and enjoy immediately.

Serving Suggestions: Serve with a topping of pomegranate seeds.
Variation Tip: Make sure to use can of pears in light syrup.
Nutritional Information per Serving:
Calories: 61 |Fat: 0.2g|Sat Fat: 0g|Carbohydrates: 16.2g|Fiber: 3.3g|Sugar: 10.4g|Protein: 0.4g

Refreshing Lemon Herb Sorbet

⏲ **Prep: 15 minutes** 🍳 **Cook: 6 minutes** 🍽 **Serves: 4**

Ingredients:

½ cup water
¼ cup granulated sugar
2 large fresh dill sprigs, stemmed
2 large fresh basil sprigs, stemmed
1 cup ice water
2 tablespoons fresh lemon juice

Preparation:

1. In a small saucepan, add the sugar and water and over medium heat and cook for about 5 minutes or until the sugar is dissolved, stirring continuously. 2. Stir in the herb sprigs and remove from the heat. 3. Add the ice water and lemon juice and stir to combine. 4. Transfer the mixture into an empty Ninja CREAMi pint container. 5. Cover the container with storage lid and freeze for 24 hours. 6. After 24 hours, remove the lid from container and arrange into the Outer Bowl of Ninja CREAMi. 7. Install the Creamerizer Paddle onto the lid of Outer Bowl. 8. Then rotate the lid clockwise to lock. 9. Press Power button to turn on the unit. 10. Then press Sorbet button. 11. When the program is completed, turn the Outer Bowl and release it from the machine. 12. Transfer the sorbet into serving bowls and serve immediately.

Serving Suggestions: Serve with the garnishing of fresh herbs.
Variation Tip: Use herbs of your choice.
Nutritional Information per Serving:
Calories: 51 | Fat: 0.1g|Sat Fat: 0g.1|Carbohydrates: 13.1g|Fiber: 0.1g|Sugar: 12.7g|Protein: 0.2g

Gooseberry Sorbet

⏲ **Prep: 10 minutes** 🍽 **Serves: 6**

Ingredients:

1 cup white caster sugar
3¾ cups gooseberry, topped and tailed
5 tablespoons undiluted elderflower cordial
1 egg white

Preparation:

1. Add all of the ingredients into a blender. Mix well until smooth. 2. Pour the mixture into the Ninja CREAMi Pint and close the lid. 3. Place the pint into the freezer and freeze for 24 hours. 4. Once done, open the lid and place the pint into the outer bowl of the Ninja CREAMi. Set the Creamerizer Paddle into the outer bowl. 5. Lock the lid by rotating it clockwise. 6. Turn the unit on and press the SORBET button. 7. Once done, take out the bowl from the Ninja CREAMi. 8. Serve and enjoy this yummy sorbet.

Serving Suggestions: Serve with some mint leaves on top.
Variation Tip: Add coconut extract for a taste variation.
Nutritional Information per Serving:
Calories: 127 | Fat: 0.4g | Sat Fat: 0.3g | Carbohydrates: 44g | Fiber: 1.2g | Sugar: 23.2g | Protein: 3.5g

Chapter 1 Sorbet

Chapter 2 Smoothie Bowls

Coconut and Berries Smoothie Bowl 20

Oats and Carrots Smoothie Bowl 20

Oat Banana Smoothie Bowl 21

Peach Chia Seeds Smoothie Bowl 21

Berries and Grapefruit Smoothie Bowl 22

Banana Coconut Smoothie Bowl 22

Delicious Papaya Orange Smoothie Bowl 23

Mango Smoothie Bowl 23

Fresh Peach & Grapefruit Smoothie Bowl 24

Melon & Pineapple Smoothie Bowl 24

Dragon Fruit Smoothie Bowl 25

Apricot Smoothie Bowl 25

Classic Blueberry Yogurt Smoothie Bowl 26

Honey Raspberry Banana Smoothie Bowl 26

Healthy Apple Cherry Smoothie Bowl 27

Strawberry & Dragon Fruit Banana Smoothie Bowl 27

Coconut and Berries Smoothie Bowl

⏱ **Prep: 10 minutes**　📚 **Serves: 2**

Ingredients:
1 cup coconut milk
½ cup berries, frozen
2 bananas, frozen
2 tablespoons sugar

Preparation:
1. Put all the ingredients into the MAX FILL line of a CREAMi pint. 2. Fasten the lid of the pint and freeze for 24 hours. 3. After 24 hours, open the pint, fix it into the outer bowl of Ninja CREAMi along with the 'Creamerizer paddle'. 4. Fasten the lid, turn on the 'Power Button', and select the 'SMOOTHIE BOWL' function. 5. Dish out the smoothie from the pint and serve as desired.

Serving Suggestions: Top with walnuts and shredded coconut.
Variation Tip: You can also use honey instead of sugar.
Nutritional Information per Serving:
Calories: 278 | Fat: 24g | Sat Fat: 21g | Carbohydrates: 7g | Fiber: 3g | Sugar: 4.3g | Protein: 2.3g

Oats and Carrots Smoothie Bowl

⏱ **Prep: 10 minutes**　🍲 **Cook: 0 minute**　📚 **Serves: 1**

Ingredients:
½ cup carrots, frozen
1 frozen banana, quartered
½ teaspoon cinnamon
¼ cup rolled oats
2 tablespoons vanilla Greek yogurt

Preparation:
1. Put the frozen carrots to the MAX FILL line of a CREAMi pint. 2. In a large bowl, merge together rolled oats, banana, vanilla Greek yogurt, and cinnamon. 3. Thoroughly blend and move the mixture in the CREAMi pint. 4. Fasten the lid of the pint and freeze for 24 hours. 5. After 24 hours, open the pint, fix it into the outer bowl of Ninja CREAMi along with the 'Creamerizer paddle'. 6. Fasten the lid, turn on the 'Power Button', and select the 'SMOOTHIE BOWL" function. 7. Dish out the smoothie from the pint and serve as desired.

Serving Suggestions: Top with caramel and sliced almonds.
Variation Tip: You can also use apples instead of carrots.
Nutritional Information per Serving:
Calories: 105 | Fat: 0.9g | Sat Fat: 0.2g | Carbohydrates: 22g | Fiber: 3g | Sugar: 8g | Protein: 2g

Oat Banana Smoothie Bowl

⏰ **Prep: 10 minutes** 🍳 **Cook: 1 minute** 🍽 **Serves: 2**

Ingredients:

¼ cup quick oats
½ cup water
1 cup vanilla Greek yogurt
3 tablespoons honey
½ cup banana, peeled and sliced

Preparation:

1. Merge the water and oats and microwave for 1 minute on High. 2. Add the yogurt, banana and honey after removing from the microwave until well combined. 3. Move this mixture to the MAX FILL line of a CREAMi pint. 4. Fasten the lid of the pint and freeze for 24 hours. 5. After 24 hours, open the pint, fix it into the outer bowl of Ninja CREAMi along with the 'Creamerizer paddle'. 6. Fasten the lid, turn on the 'Power Button', and select the 'SMOOTHIE BOWL' function. 7. Dish out the smoothie from the pint and serve as desired.

Serving Suggestions: Serve with the topping of peanuts, banana, and granola.

Variation Tip: You can use some other nuts too.

Nutritional Information per Serving:
Calories: 278 | Fat: 2.7g | Sat Fat: 1.1g | Carbohydrates: 55.7g | Fiber: 2.1g | Sugar: 41.6g | Protein: 10.9g

Peach Chia Seeds Smoothie Bowl

⏰ **Prep: 10 minutes** 🍽 **Serves: 1**

Ingredients:

1 cup almond milk, unsweetened
1 cup ice
1 scoop vanilla protein
½ cup peaches, frozen
1 tablespoon chia seeds

Preparation:

1. In a blender, blitz all the ingredients until smooth. 2. Move this mixture to the MAX FILL line of a CREAMi pint. 3. Fasten the lid of the pint and freeze for 24 hours. 4. After 24 hours, open the pint, fix it into the outer bowl of Ninja CREAMi along with the 'Creamerizer paddle'. 5. Fasten the lid, turn on the 'Power Button', and select the 'SMOOTHIE BOWL' function. 6. Dish out the smoothie from the pint and serve as desired.

Serving Suggestions: Serve topped with peach slices, whipped cream, and walnuts.

Variation Tip: You can use coconut milk or even regular milk.

Nutritional Information per Serving:
Calories: 490 | Fat: 37g | Sat Fat: 30g | Carbohydrates: 21g | Fiber: 6g | Sugar: 15g | Protein: 5g

Berries and Grapefruit Smoothie Bowl

⏱ **Prep: 5 minutes** 🍽 **Serves: 1**

Ingredients:

2 cups frozen berries
½ cup grapefruit juice
1 tablespoon sugar

Preparation:

1. In a large bowl, merge together the berries, grapefruit juice, and sugar. 2. Move this mixture to the MAX FILL line of a CREAMi pint. 3. Fasten the lid of the pint and freeze for 24 hours. 4. After 24 hours, open the pint, fix it into the outer bowl of Ninja CREAMi along with the 'Creamerizer paddle'. 5. Fasten the lid, turn on the 'Power Button', and select the 'SMOOTHIE BOWL' function. 6. Dish out the smoothie from the pint and serve as desired.

Serving Suggestions: Top with berries and shredded coconut.
Variation Tip: You can use honey or stevia instead of sugar.
Nutritional Information per Serving:
Calories: 102 | Fat: 0.1g | Sat Fat: 0g | Carbohydrates: 30g | Fiber: 5g | Sugar: 22g | Protein: 1.2g

Banana Coconut Smoothie Bowl

⏱ **Prep: 10 minutes** 🍽 **Serves: 2**

Ingredients:

½ of ripe banana, peeled and cut in ½-inch pieces
¼ cup coconut rum
¼ cup coconut cream
½ cup unsweetened canned coconut milk
¾ cup pineapple juice
2 tablespoons fresh lime juice

Preparation:

1. In a large-sized bowl, add banana and remaining ingredients and whisk until blended thoroughly. 2. Transfer the blended mixture into an empty Ninja CREAMi pint container. 3. Cover the container with a storage lid and freeze for 24 hours. 4. After 24 hours, remove the lid from the container and arrange it into the outer bowl of Ninja CREAMi. 5. Install the "Creamerizer Paddle" onto the lid of the outer bowl. 6. Then rotate the lid clockwise to lock. 7. Press "Power" button to turn on the unit. 8. Then press "SMOOTHIE BOWL" button. 9. When the program is completed, turn the outer bowl and release it from the machine. 10. Transfer the smoothie into serving bowls and enjoy immediately.

Serving Suggestions: Serve with a topping of granola.
Variation Tip: Swap rum for other spirits such as vodka or tequila.
Nutritional Information per Serving:
Calories: 301 |Fat: 15.6g|Sat Fat: 13.9g|Carbohydrates: 22.1g|Fiber: 1.6g|Sugar: 15.5g|Protein: 2.1g

Delicious Papaya Orange Smoothie Bowl

⏲ **Prep: 10 minutes** ⬙ **Serves: 2**

Ingredients:

1 cup frozen papaya chunks
1 cup plain Greek yogurt
¼ cup fresh orange juice
2 tablespoons maple syrup
½ teaspoon ground cinnamon

Preparation:

1. In a high-powered blender, add papaya and remaining ingredients and process until smooth. 2. Transfer the blended mixture into an empty Ninja CREAMi pint container. 3. Cover the container with storage lid and freeze for 24 hours. 4. After 24 hours, remove the lid from container and arrange into the outer bowl of Ninja CREAMi. 5. Install the "Creamerizer Paddle" onto the lid of outer bowl. 6. Then rotate the lid clockwise to lock. 7. Press "Power" button to turn on the unit. 8. Then press "SMOOTHIE BOWL" button. 9. When the program is completed, turn the outer bowl and release it from the machine. 10. Transfer the smoothie into serving bowls and enjoy immediately.

Serving Suggestions: Drizzle the smoothie bowl with honey before serving.
Variation Tip: To make the smoothie bowl more filling, add a scoop of protein powder.
Nutritional Information per Serving:
Calories: 186 |Fat: 1.8g|Sat Fat: 1.3g|Carbohydrates: 33.6g|Fiber: 1.6g|Sugar: 28.8g|Protein: 7.6g

Mango Smoothie Bowl

⏲ **Prep: 10 minutes** ⬙ **Serves: 2**

Ingredients:

2 cups ripe mango, peeled and cut into 1-inch pieces
14 ounces coconut milk
2-3 drops liquid stevia
¼ teaspoon vanilla extract

Preparation:

1. Place the mango pieces into an empty Ninja CREAMi pint container. 2. Top with coconut milk, stevia and vanilla extract and stir to combine. 3. Cover the container with the storage lid and freeze for 24 hours. 4. After 24 hours, remove the lid from container and arrange into the outer bowl of Ninja CREAMi. 5. Install the "Creamerizer Paddle" onto the lid of outer bowl. 6. Then rotate the lid clockwise to lock. 7. Press "Power" button to turn on the unit. 8. Then press "SMOOTHIE BOWL" button. 9. When the program is completed, turn the outer bowl and release it from the machine. 10. Transfer the smoothie into serving bowls and enjoy immediately.

Serving Suggestions: Serve with a topping of coconut flakes.
Variation Tip: Coconut milk can be replaced with non-dairy milk too.
Nutritional Information per Serving:
Calories: 220 |Fat: 7.1g|Sat Fat: 3.9g|Carbohydrates: 33.8g|Fiber: 2.6g|Sugar: 33.1g|Protein: 7.7g

Fresh Peach & Grapefruit Smoothie Bowl

Prep: 10 minutes   Serves: 2

Ingredients:
1 cup frozen peach pieces
1 cup vanilla Greek yogurt
¼ cup fresh grapefruit juice
2 tablespoons honey
¼ teaspoon vanilla extract
½ teaspoon ground cinnamon

Preparation:
1. In a high-powered blender, add peach pieces and remaining ingredients and process until smooth. 2. Transfer the blended mixture into an empty Ninja CREAMi pint container. 3. Cover the container with storage lid and freeze for 24 hours. 4. After 24 hours, remove the lid from container and arrange into the outer bowl of Ninja CREAMi. 5. Install the "Creamerizer Paddle" onto the lid of outer bowl. 6. Then rotate the lid clockwise to lock. 7. Press "Power" button to turn on the unit. 8. Then press "SMOOTHIE BOWL" button. 9. When the program is completed, turn the outer bowl and release it from the machine. 10. Transfer the smoothie into serving bowls and enjoy immediately.

Serving Suggestions: Serve with a sprinkling of chia seeds.
Variation Tip: Blend in some ginger or turmeric for a spicy twist.
Nutritional Information per Serving:
Calories: 197 |Fat: 1.8g|Sat Fat: 1.2g|Carbohydrates: 36.7g|Fiber: 1.6g|Sugar: 35.6g|Protein: 8g

Melon & Pineapple Smoothie Bowl

Prep: 10 minutes   Serves: 2

Ingredients:
3½ ounces melon chunks
3½ ounces pineapple chunks
5¼ ounces vanilla yogurt
3½ fluid ounces whole milk

Preparation:
1. Place the melon and pineapple chunks into an empty Ninja CREAMi pint container and stir to combine. 2. Top with yogurt and milk. 3. Cover the container with storage lid and freeze for 24 hours. 4. After 24 hours, remove the lid from container and arrange into the outer bowl of Ninja CREAMi. 5. Install the "Creamerizer Paddle" onto the lid of outer bowl. 6. Then rotate the lid clockwise to lock. 7. Press "Power" button to turn on the unit. 8. Then press "SMOOTHIE BOWL" button. 9. When the program is completed, turn the outer bowl and release it from the machine. 10. Transfer the smoothie into serving bowls and enjoy immediately.

Serving Suggestions: Serve with a drizzling of maple syrup.
Variation Tip: Add a sprinkle of cinnamon for a warm flavor.
Nutritional Information per Serving:
Calories: 334 |Fat: 8.1g|Sat Fat: 4.8g|Carbohydrates: 46.5g|Fiber: 6.1g|Sugar: 28.9g|Protein: 27.2g

Dragon Fruit Smoothie Bowl

⏲ Prep: 10 minutes ⬧ Serves: 4

Ingredients:
2 cups frozen dragon fruit chunks
2 (6-ounces) cans pineapple juice

Preparation:
1. Place the dragon fruit chunks into an empty Ninja CREAMi pint container. 2. Top with pineapple juice and stir to combine. 3. Cover the container with storage lid and freeze for 24 hours. 4. After 24 hours, remove the lid from container and arrange into the Outer Bowl of Ninja CREAMi. 5. Install the Creamerizer Paddle onto the lid of Outer Bowl. 6. Then rotate the lid clockwise to lock. 7. Press Power button to turn on the unit. 8. Then press Smoothie Bowl button. 9. When the program is completed, turn the Outer Bowl and release it from the machine. 10. Transfer the smoothie into serving bowls and serve immediately.

Serving Suggestions: Serve with the topping of fruit, chia seeds and granola.

Variation Tip: If you like sweeter smoothie, then use some sweetener.

Nutritional Information per Serving:
Calories: 68 | Fat: 0.1g|Sat Fat: 0g|Carbohydrates: 17g|Fiber: 0.2g|Sugar: 14.5g|Protein: 0.3g

Apricot Smoothie Bowl

⏲ Prep: 10 minutes ⬧ Serves: 3

Ingredients:
1 (14-ounce) can unsweetened coconut milk
2 cups apricots, pitted and cut into 1-inch pieces

Preparation:
1. Place the apricot pieces into the Ninja CREAMi Pint. 2. Top with the coconut milk and stir to combine. 3. Snap the lid on the pint and freeze it for 24 hours. 4. Remove the lid and assemble the unit as per the user instructions. 5. Select the SMOOTHIE BOWL program. 6. When the program is complete, remove the outer bowl. 7. Transfer the smoothie into serving bowls and serve immediately.

Serving Suggestions: Serve with a topping of apricot chunks and granola.

Variation Tip: Add a drizzle of honey.

Nutritional Information per Serving:
Calories: 354 | Fat: 32.2g | Sat Fat: 28g | Carbohydrates: 18.7g |Fiber: 4.9g | Sugar: 13.8g | Protein: 4.4g

Chapter 2 Smoothie Bowls

Classic Blueberry Yogurt Smoothie Bowl

Prep: 10 minutes   Serves: 2

Ingredients:
2 cups fresh blueberries
½ cup plain yogurt
¼ cup fresh orange juice
1 tablespoon maple syrup

Preparation:
1. In an empty Ninja CREAMi pint container, put in the blueberries and with the back of a spoon, firmly press the berries below the MAX FILL line. 2. Put in yogurt, orange juice and maple syrup and blend to incorporate. 3. Cover the container with storage lid and freeze for 24 hours. 4. After 24 hours, take off the lid from container and arrange into the outer bowl of Ninja CREAMi. 5. Install the "Creamerizer Paddle" onto the lid of outer bowl. 6. Then rotate the lid clockwise to lock. 7. Press "Power" button to turn on the unit. 8. Then press "SMOOTHIE BOWL" button. 9. When the program is completed, turn the outer bowl and release it from the machine. 10. Transfer the smoothie into serving bowls and enjoy immediately.

Serving Suggestions: Serve with a topping of coconut.
Variation Tip: Use best quality blueberries.
Nutritional Information per Serving:
Calories: 167 |Fat: 1.3g|Sat Fat: 0.6g|Carbohydrates: 35.2g|Fiber: 3.6g|Sugar: 27.3g|Protein: 4.8g

Honey Raspberry Banana Smoothie Bowl

Prep: 10 minutes   Serves: 4

Ingredients:
2 tablespoons vanilla protein powder
¼ cup honey
¼ cup orange juice
½ cup coconut milk
1 cup banana, peel removed and cut in ½-inch pieces
1 cup fresh raspberries

Preparation:
1. In a large-sized bowl, put in protein powder, honey, apple juice and coconut milk and whisk to incorporate thoroughly. 2. Place the banana and raspberries into an empty Ninja CREAMi pint container and with the back of a spoon, firmly press the fruit below the MAX FILL line. 3. Top with milk mixture and blend to incorporate thoroughly. 4. Cover the container with storage lid and freeze for 24 hours. 5. After 24 hours, take off the lid from container and arrange into the outer bowl of Ninja CREAMi. 6. Install the "Creamerizer Paddle" onto the lid of outer bowl. 7. Then rotate the lid clockwise to lock. 8. Press "Power" button to turn on the unit. 9. Then press "SMOOTHIE BOWL" button. 10. When the program is completed, turn the outer bowl and release it from the machine. 11. Transfer the smoothie into serving bowls and enjoy immediately.

Serving Suggestions: Serve with a topping of fresh berries.
Variation Tip: You can use protein powder according to your liking.
Nutritional Information per Serving:
Calories: 288 |Fat: 16.2g|Sat Fat: 13.8g|Carbohydrates: 32g|Fiber: 7.6g|Sugar: 16.8g|Protein: 9.2g

Healthy Apple Cherry Smoothie Bowl

⏱ Prep: 10 minutes   🍴 Serves: 2

Ingredients:
2 cups frozen cherries
1 cup apple juice
⅓ cup maple syrup
½ teaspoon ground cinnamon

Preparation:
1. In an empty Ninja CREAMi pint container, put in cherries. 2. In a large-sized bowl, put in the apple juice, maple syrup and cinnamon and whisk until blended thoroughly. 3. Place the blended mixture over the cherries and lightly blend to incorporate. 4. Cover the container with storage lid and freeze for 24 hours. 5. After 24 hours, take off the lid from container and arrange into the outer bowl of Ninja CREAMi. 6. Install the "Creamerizer Paddle" onto the lid of outer bowl. 7. Then rotate the lid clockwise to lock. 8. Press "Power" button to turn on the unit. 9. Then press "SMOOTHIE BOWL" button. 10. When the program is completed, turn the outer bowl and release it from the machine. 11. Transfer the smoothie into serving bowls and enjoy immediately.

Serving Suggestions: Serve with a topping of granola.
Variation Tip: maple syrup can be replaced with honey.
Nutritional Information per Serving:
Calories: 285 |Fat: 0.3g|Sat Fat: 0.1g|Carbohydrates: 71.7g|Fiber: 3.6g|Sugar: 62.3g|Protein: 2.1g

Strawberry & Dragon Fruit Banana Smoothie Bowl

⏱ Prep: 10 minutes   🍴 Serves: 2

Ingredients:
½ cup coconut water
2 cups frozen dragon fruit, chopped
2 cup frozen strawberries, hulled
1 banana, peeled
1-2 tablespoons honey

Preparation:
1. In a high-powered blender, put in water and remaining ingredients and process to form a smooth mixture. 2. Transfer the blended mixture into an empty Ninja CREAMi pint container. 3. Cover the container with storage lid and freeze for 24 hours. 4. After 24 hours, take off the lid from container and arrange into the outer bowl of Ninja CREAMi. 5. Install the "Creamerizer Paddle" onto the lid of outer bowl. 6. Then rotate the lid clockwise to lock. 7. Press "Power" button to turn on the unit. 8. Then press "SMOOTHIE BOWL" button. 9. When the program is completed, turn the outer bowl and release it from the machine. 10. Transfer the smoothie into serving bowls and enjoy immediately.

Serving Suggestions: Serve with a topping of banana and strawberry slices.
Variation Tip: You can use maple water instead of coconut water.
Nutritional Information per Serving:
Calories: 187 |Fat: 0.7g|Sat Fat: 0.2g|Carbohydrates: 47.6g|Fiber: 5.1g|Sugar: 36.5g|Protein: 2.1g

Chapter 3 Milkshake

Hazelnut Chocolate Milkshake ………………………………… 29

Chocolate Banana Milkshake ………………………………… 29

Vanilla Marshmallow Oat Milkshake ………………………… 30

Pumpkin Coffee Milkshake…………………………………… 30

Cashew Chocolate Banana Milkshake ……………………… 31

Flavorful Sugar Cookie Vanilla Milkshake…………………… 31

Amaretto Chocolate Cookies Milkshake …………………… 32

Almond Milkshake …………………………………………… 32

Vanilla Ice Cream Milkshake ………………………………… 33

Vanilla Oreo Milkshake ……………………………………… 33

Chocolate Cookie Milkshake ………………………………… 34

Coffee Ice Cream Milkshake ………………………………… 34

Strawberry Shortcake Milkshake …………………………… 35

Pistachio Milkshake …………………………………………… 35

Blueberry Milkshake ………………………………………… 36

Raspberry Ice Cream Milkshake……………………………… 36

Hazelnut Chocolate Milkshake

⏰ Prep: 5 minutes   🍽 Serves: 2

Ingredients:
1½ cups hazelnut ice cream
½ cup whole milk
¼ cup chocolate spread

Preparation:
1. Move all the ingredients into a CREAMi pint container and merge well. 2. Fasten the lid of the pint and freeze for 24 hours. 3. After 24 hours, open the pint, fix it into the outer bowl of Ninja CREAMi along with the 'Creamerizer paddle'. 4. Fasten the lid, turn on the 'Power Button', and select the 'MILKSHAKE' function. 5. Ladle out the shake into serving glasses and serve chilled.

Serving Suggestions: Serve with the sprinkling of cocoa powder.
Variation Tip: You can use milk of your choice.
Nutritional Information per Serving:
Calories: 209 | Fat: 11g | Sat Fat: 5g | Carbohydrates: 21g | Fiber: 0.8g | Sugar: 20g | Protein: 4g

Chocolate Banana Milkshake

⏰ Prep: 2 minutes   🍳 Cook: 0 minute   🍽 Serves: 2

Ingredients:
½ cup cashew milk
1½ cups vegan chocolate ice cream
½ cup fresh banana, ripe
1 tablespoon coffee powder, instant

Preparation:
1. Move the ice cream into a CREAMi pint container. 2. Use a spoon to make a hole that is 1½ inches wide in the pint's bottom. 3. Add the remaining ingredients to the hole. 4. Fasten the lid of the pint and freeze for 24 hours. 5. After 24 hours, open the pint, fix it into the outer bowl of Ninja CREAMi along with the 'Creamerizer paddle'. 6. Fasten the lid, turn on the 'Power Button', and select the 'MILKSHAKE' function. 7. Ladle out the shake into serving glasses and serve chilled.

Serving Suggestions: Serve topped with chocolate.
Variation Tip: You can use almond or coconut milk too.
Nutritional Information per Serving:
Calories: 142 | Fat: 5.9g | Sat Fat: 3.4g | Carbohydrates: 20g | Fiber: 1g | Sugar: 15g | Protein: 2g

Vanilla Marshmallow Oat Milkshake

Prep: 10 minutes **Serves: 2**

Ingredients:
1½ cups vanilla ice cream
½ cup oat milk
½ cup marshmallow cereal

Preparation:
1. Move the ice cream, oat milk, and marshmallow cereal into a CREAMi pint container. 2. Fasten the lid of the pint and freeze for 24 hours. 3. After 24 hours, open the pint, fix it into the outer bowl of Ninja CREAMi along with the 'Creamerizer paddle'. 4. Fasten the lid, turn on the 'Power Button', and select the 'MILKSHAKE' function. 5. Ladle out the shake into serving glasses and serve chilled.

Serving Suggestions: Serve topped with whipped cream and mini marshmallows.
Variation Tip: You can use almond milk too.
Nutritional Information per Serving:
Calories: 165 | Fat: 6.1g | Sat Fat: 3.5g | Carbohydrates: 24.8g | Fiber: 1.1g | Sugar: 19.3g | Protein: 3g

Pumpkin Coffee Milkshake

Prep: 5 minutes **Serves: 4**

Ingredients:
2 cups whole milk
2 tablespoons sugar, granulated
1 cup coffee, brewed
4 cups vanilla ice cream
½ cup pumpkin puree, canned
1 teaspoon pumpkin pie spice
2 teaspoons vanilla extract
1 cup ice cubes

Preparation:
1. In a saucepan, lightly boil the milk and then ladle out in a mixing bowl. 2. Merge in the pumpkin, sugar, pumpkin pie spice, coffee, and vanilla essence. 3. Whisk well and refrigerate for an hour. 4. Move the mixture into a CREAMi pint container along with vanilla ice cream. 5. Fasten the lid of the pint and freeze for 24 hours. 6. After 24 hours, open the pint, fix it into the outer bowl of Ninja CREAMi along with the 'Creamerizer paddle'. 7. Fasten the lid, turn on the 'Power Button', and select the 'MILKSHAKE' function. 8. Ladle out the shake into serving glasses and serve chilled.

Serving Suggestions: Top with caramel and whipped cream
Variation Tip: You can also add caramel ice cream.
Nutritional Information per Serving:
Calories: 260 | Fat: 11g | Sat Fat: 6g | Carbohydrates: 30g | Fiber: 1g | Sugar:27 g | Protein: 6 g

Cashew Chocolate Banana Milkshake

⏲ **Prep: 5 minutes** ≡ **Serves: 2**

Ingredients:

½ cup cashew milk
1½ cups chocolate ice cream
½ cup ripe banana, cut into pieces
1 tablespoon instant coffee powder

Preparation:

1. Move all the ingredients into a CREAMi pint container except the chocolate chip cookies. 2. Fasten the lid of the pint and freeze for 24 hours. 3. After 24 hours, open the pint, fix it into the outer bowl of Ninja CREAMi along with the 'Creamerizer paddle'. 4. Fasten the lid, turn on the 'Power Button', and select the 'MILKSHAKE' function. 5. Ladle out the shake into serving glasses and serve chilled.

Serving Suggestions: Serve garnished with pistachios.
Variation Tip: You can also use vanilla ice cream.
Nutritional Information per Serving:
Calories: 269 | Fat: 12g | Sat Fat: 7.7g | Carbohydrates: 40g | Fiber: 2.4g | Sugar: 32g | Protein: 4g

Flavorful Sugar Cookie Vanilla Milkshake

⏲ **Prep: 10 minutes** ≡ **Serves: 2**

Ingredients:

1 cup vanilla ice cream
1 cup oat milk
2 small sugar cookies, crushed
4 tablespoons sprinkles

Preparation:

1. In an empty Ninja CREAMi pint container, place the ice cream. 2. With a spoon, create a 1½-inch wide hole in the center that reaches the bottom of the pint container. 3. Add the remaining ingredients into the hole. 4. Arrange the container into the outer bowl of Ninja CREAMi. 5. Install the "Creamerizer Paddle" onto the lid of outer bowl. 6. Then rotate the lid clockwise to lock. 7. Press "Power" button to turn on the unit. 8. Then press "MILKSHAKE" button. 9. When the program is completed, turn the outer bowl and release it from the machine. 10. Transfer the shake into serving glasses and enjoy immediately.

Serving Suggestions: Top your milkshake some festive sprinkles.
Variation Tip: You can add a splash of liqueur such as Kahlua, or rum.
Nutritional Information per Serving:
Calories: 212 |Fat: 8.3g|Sat Fat: 4.3g|Carbohydrates: 34.2g|Fiber: 5.1g|Sugar: 23g|Protein: 4.3g

Chapter 3 Milkshake | 31

Amaretto Chocolate Cookies Milkshake

⏱ Prep: 10 minutes   🍽 Serves: 2

Ingredients:

1 cup whole milk
½ cup amaretto-flavored coffee creamer
¼ cup amaretto liqueur
1 tablespoon agave nectar
¼ cup chocolate chip cookies, chopped

Preparation:

1. In an empty Ninja CREAMi pint container, place milk and remaining ingredients except for cookies and stir to combine. 2. Cover the container with the storage lid and freeze for 24 hours. 3. After 24 hours, remove the lid from container and arrange into the outer bowl of Ninja CREAMi. 4. Install the "Creamerizer Paddle" onto the lid of outer bowl. 5. Then rotate the lid clockwise to lock. 6. Press "Power" button to turn on the unit. 7. Then press "MILKSHAKE" button. 8. When the program is completed, turn the outer bowl and release it from the machine. 9. Transfer the shake into serving glasses and sprinkle with chopped chocolate chip cookies, enjoy immediately.

Serving Suggestions: Serve the milkshake with a dusting of cinnamon for a warm flavor.

Variation Tip: Instead of chocolate chip cookies, try using amaretto cookies.

Nutritional Information per Serving:

Calories: 371 |Fat: 17.6g|Sat Fat: 9.5g|Carbohydrates: 25.9g|Fiber: 1g|Sugar: 42.2g|Protein: 6.5g

Almond Milkshake

⏱ Prep: 10 minutes   🍽 Serves: 2

Ingredients:

1½ cups vanilla ice cream
½ cup unsweetened almond milk
2 tablespoons honey
¼ cup almonds, chopped
½ teaspoon ground cinnamon
¼ teaspoon vanilla extract

Preparation:

1. In an empty Ninja CREAMi pint container, place ice cream, followed by almond milk, honey, almonds, cinnamon and vanilla extract. 2. Arrange the container into the outer bowl of Ninja CREAMi. 3. Install the "Creamerizer Paddle" onto the lid of outer bowl. 4. Then rotate the lid clockwise to lock. 5. Press "Power" button to turn on the unit. 6. Then press "MILKSHAKE" button. 7. When the program is completed, turn the outer bowl and release it from the machine. 8. Transfer the shake into serving glasses and enjoy immediately.

Serving Suggestions: Serve with a topping of some chopped almonds for a nutty crunch.

Variation Tip: Use almond butter instead of almonds for a richer, creamier consistency.

Nutritional Information per Serving:

Calories: 248 |Fat: 12.1g|Sat Fat: 3.9g|Carbohydrates: 32.9g|Fiber: 2.5g|Sugar: 28.3g|Protein: 4.6g

Vanilla Ice Cream Milkshake

Prep: 10 minutes **Serves: 2**

Ingredients:

2 cups vanilla ice cream
1 cup whole milk
1 teaspoon vanilla extract

Preparation:

1. In an empty Ninja CREAMi pint container, place the ice cream. 2. Top with the milk and vanilla extract and gently stir to combine. 3. Arrange the container into the outer bowl of Ninja CREAMi. 4. Install the "Creamerizer Paddle" onto the lid of outer bowl. 5. Then rotate the lid clockwise to lock. 6. Press "Power" button to turn on the unit. 7. Then press "MILKSHAKE" button. 8. When the program is completed, turn the outer bowl and release it from the machine. 9. Transfer the shake into serving glasses and enjoy immediately.

Serving Suggestions: Serve with a topping of rainbow sprinkles.
Variation Tip: Vanilla bean paste can be used instead of vanilla extract.
Nutritional Information per Serving:
Calories: 216 |Fat: 11g|Sat Fat: 6.8g|Carbohydrates: 21.8g|Fiber: 0.5g|Sugar: 20.7g|Protein: 6.2g

Vanilla Oreo Milkshake

Prep: 10 minutes **Serves: 2**

Ingredients:

2 cups vanilla ice cream
⅔ cup milk
8 Oreo cookies, crushed
1 teaspoon vanilla extract

Preparation:

1. In an empty Ninja CREAMi pint container, place the ice cream. 2. Top with the remaining ingredients and gently stir to combine. 3. Arrange the container into the outer bowl of Ninja CREAMi. 4. Install the "Creamerizer Paddle" onto the lid of outer bowl. 5. Then rotate the lid clockwise to lock. 6. Press "Power" button to turn on the unit. 7. Then press "MILKSHAKE" button. 8. When the program is completed, turn the outer bowl and release it from the machine. 9. Transfer the shake into serving glasses and enjoy immediately.

Serving Suggestions: Serve with a topping of whipped cream.
Variation Tip: Start with the best ingredients.
Nutritional Information per Serving:
Calories: 370 |Fat: 16.3g|Sat Fat: 7g|Carbohydrates: 48.9g|Fiber: 1.7g|Sugar: 34.2g|Protein: 7.1g

Chocolate Cookie Milkshake

⏲ **Prep: 10 minutes** 🍽 **Serves: 2**

Ingredients:

1½ cups cookie n' cream ice cream
½ cup whole milk
2 tablespoons cream cheese, softened
3 chocolate sandwich cookies, crushed

Preparation:

1. In an empty Ninja CREAMi pint container, place the ice cream. 2. Top with the remaining ingredients and gently stir to combine. 3. Arrange the container into the outer bowl of Ninja CREAMi. 4. Install the "Creamerizer Paddle" onto the lid of outer bowl. 5. Then rotate the lid clockwise to lock. 6. Press "Power" button to turn on the unit. 7. Then press "MILKSHAKE" button. 8. When the program is completed, turn the outer bowl and release it from the machine. 9. Transfer the shake into serving glasses and enjoy immediately.

Serving Suggestions: Serve with a sprinkling of chocolate shavings.
Variation Tip: Serve with a topping of extra sprinkles
Nutritional Information per Serving:
Calories: 339 |Fat: 18.2g|Sat Fat: 8.2g|Carbohydrates: 42g|Fiber: 0.4g|Sugar: 13.7g|Protein: 6g

Coffee Ice Cream Milkshake

⏲ **Prep: 10 minutes** 🍽 **Serves: 2**

Ingredients:

1½ cups coffee ice cream
½ cup whole milk

Preparation:

1. In an empty Ninja CREAMi pint container, place the ice cream, followed by milk. 2. Arrange the container into the outer bowl of Ninja CREAMi. 3. Install the "Creamerizer Paddle" onto the lid of outer bowl. 4. Then rotate the lid clockwise to lock. 5. Press "Power" button to turn on the unit. 6. Then press "MILKSHAKE" button. 7. When the program is completed, turn the outer bowl and release it from the machine. 8. Transfer the shake into serving glasses and enjoy immediately.

Serving Suggestions: Serve with a topping of whipped cream.
Variation Tip: Use the best quality ice cream.
Nutritional Information per Serving:
Calories: 142 |Fat: 7.2g|Sat Fat: 4.5g|Carbohydrates: 14g|Fiber: 0g|Sugar: 14.5g|Protein: 4.2g

Strawberry Shortcake Milkshake

⏰ **Prep: 2 minutes**   📚 **Serves: 2**

Ingredients:

1½ cups strawberry ice cream
½ cup whole milk
¼ premade pound cake, crumbled
¼ cup fresh strawberries, trimmed, cut in quarters

Preparation:

1. Fill an empty CREAMi Pint with the ice cream. 2. Create a 1-inch wide hole in the bottom of the pint using a spoon. Fill the hole with the remaining ingredients. 3. Arrange the container into the outer bowl of the Ninja CREAMi. 4. Install the Creamerizer Paddle onto the lid of the outer bowl, then rotate the lid clockwise to lock. 5. Turn the unit on. 6. Press the MILKSHAKE button. 7. When the program is complete, turn the outer bowl and release it from the machine. 8. Transfer the shake into serving glasses and serve immediately.

Serving Suggestions: Serve with a garnishing of fresh berries.
Variation Tip: You can use any milk you prefer.
Nutritional Information per Serving:
Calories: 347 | Fat: 14g | Sat Fat: 4g | Carbohydrates: 34g | Fiber: 0.9g | Sugar: 13g | Protein: 5g

Pistachio Milkshake

⏰ **Prep: 10 minutes**   📚 **Serves: 2**

Ingredients:

1½ cups vanilla ice cream
½ cup whole milk
2 tablespoons maple syrup
¼ cup pistachios, chopped
¼ teaspoon vanilla extract

Preparation:

1. In an empty Ninja CREAMi pint container, put in ice cream, followed by milk, maple syrup, pistachios and vanilla extract. 2. Arrange the container into the outer bowl of Ninja CREAMi. 3. Install the "Creamerizer Paddle" onto the lid of outer bowl. 4. Then rotate the lid clockwise to lock. 5. Press "Power" button to turn on the unit. 6. Then press "MILKSHAKE" button. 7. When the program is completed, turn the outer bowl and release it from the machine. 8. Transfer the shake into serving glasses and enjoy immediately.

Serving Suggestions: Serve with a topping of whipped cream.
Variation Tip: Feel free to use ice cream of your choice.
Nutritional Information per Serving:
Calories: 233 |Fat: 10.8g|Sat Fat: 4.9g|Carbohydrates: 30.3g|Fiber: 1.1g|Sugar: 26.2g|Protein: 5.2g

Blueberry Milkshake

⏱ **Prep: 10 minutes** 🍧 **Serves: 2**

Ingredients:

1½ ounces vanilla ice cream
5¼ ounces fresh blueberries
3 ounces full-fat coconut milk
Dash of vanilla extract

Preparation:

1. In an empty Ninja CREAMi pint container, put in the ice cream. 2. Top with the blueberries, coconut milk and vanilla extract and lightly blend to incorporate. 3. Arrange the container into the outer bowl of Ninja CREAMi. 4. Install the "Creamerizer Paddle" onto the lid of outer bowl. 5. Then rotate the lid clockwise to lock. 6. Press "Power" button to turn on the unit. 7. Then press "MILKSHAKE" button. 8. When the program is completed, turn the outer bowl and release it from the machine. 9. Transfer the shake into serving glasses and enjoy immediately.

Serving Suggestions: Serve with a garnishing of fresh blueberries.
Variation Tip: Make sure to use full-fat coconut milk.
Nutritional Information per Serving:
Calories: 310 |Fat: 22g|Sat Fat: 19.9g|Carbohydrates: 24.3g|Fiber: 2.2g|Sugar: 17.9g|Protein: 3.8g

Raspberry Ice Cream Milkshake

⏱ **Prep: 10 minutes** 🍧 **Serves: 2**

Ingredients:

1½ cups raspberry ice cream
½ cup whole milk

Preparation:

1. In an empty Ninja CREAMi pint container, put in ice cream, followed by milk. 2. Arrange the container into the outer bowl of Ninja CREAMi. 3. Install the "Creamerizer Paddle" onto the lid of outer bowl. 4. Then rotate the lid clockwise to lock. 5. Press "Power" button to turn on the unit. 6. Then press "MILKSHAKE" button. 7. When the program is completed, turn the outer bowl and release it from the machine. 8. Transfer the shake into serving glasses and enjoy immediately.

Serving Suggestions: Serve with a topping of whipped cream.
Variation Tip: Use best quality raspberry ice cream.
Nutritional Information per Serving:
Calories: 139 |Fat: 7.2g|Sat Fat: 4.5g|Carbohydrates: 14.8g|Fiber: 0.4g|Sugar: 13.7g|Protein: 3.7g

Chapter 4 Ice Creams

Walnut Ice Cream 38

Refreshing Lime Avocado Ice Cream 38

Chocolate Chip Cracker Ice Cream 39

Cherry Ice Cream 39

Sea Salt Caramel Ice Cream 40

Coconut Ice Cream 40

Delicious Caramel Ice Cream 41

Banana Ice Cream 41

Vanilla Peach Ice Cream 42

Banana Pineapple Rum Ice Cream 42

Pumpkin Brown Sugar Ice Cream 43

Mocha Ice Cream 43

Pear Ice Cream 44

Blackberry Ice Cream 44

Walnut Ice Cream

⏰ Prep: 10 minutes 🍴 Serves: 4

Ingredients:
1 cup whole milk
3 tablespoons walnut paste, smooth
1 tablespoon heavy whipped cream
1 teaspoon vanilla extract

Preparation:
1. In a large bowl, merge together all the ingredients until combined. 2. Move the mixture into an empty Ninja CREAMI pint. 3. Fasten the lid of the pint and freeze for 24 hours. 4. After 24 hours, open the pint, fix it into the outer bowl of Ninja CREAMi along with the 'Creamerizer paddle'. 5. Fasten the lid, turn on the 'Power Button', and select the 'ICE CREAM' function. 6. Dish out the ice cream from the pint and serve chilled.

Serving Suggestions: Serve topped with walnuts and caramel sauce.
Variation Tip: You can also use skim or nut milk.
Nutritional Information per Serving:
Calories: 90 | Fat: 8g | Sat Fat: 3g | Carbohydrates: 8g | Fiber: 0g | Sugar: 5g | Protein: 2g

Refreshing Lime Avocado Ice Cream

⏰ Prep: 10 minutes 🍴 Serves: 4

Ingredients:
1 (13½-ounce) can full-fat coconut milk
2 avocados, peeled and pitted
1 cup maple syrup
1 tablespoon lime zest
½ cup fresh lime juice
¼ cup water

Preparation:
1. In a large-sized high-powered blender, add all of the ingredients and process until smooth. 2. Transfer the blended mixture into an empty Ninja CREAMi pint container. 3. Cover the container with storage lid and freeze for 24 hours. 4. After 24 hours, remove the lid from container and arrange into the outer bowl of Ninja CREAMi. 5. Install the "Creamerizer Paddle" onto the lid of outer bowl. 6. Then rotate the lid clockwise to lock. 7. Press "Power" button to turn on the unit. 8. Then press "ICE CREAM" button. 9. When the program is completed, turn the outer bowl and release it from the machine. 10. Transfer the ice cream into serving bowls and enjoy immediately.

Serving Suggestions: Serve topped with whipped cream.
Variation Tip: You can add some cream.
Nutritional Information per Serving:
Calories: 411 |Fat: 37.3g|Sat Fat: 20.3g|Carbohydrates: 18.9g|Fiber: 6.9g|Sugar: 2g|Protein: 3.4g

Chocolate Chip Cracker Ice Cream

⏲ **Prep: 15 minutes** ◈ **Cook: 35 minutes** **Serves: 6**

Ingredients:

½ cup Buncha Crunch
½ teaspoon vanilla extract
1½ cups heavy cream
¼ teaspoon xanthan gum
½ teaspoon salt
½ cup mini chocolate chips
1 tablespoon corn syrup
1½ cups whole milk
8 graham crackers, crushed
½ cup light brown sugar

Preparation:

1. In a bowl, merge the brown sugar with graham crackers, salt, and xanthan gum. 2. In a saucepan, cook the milk, cream, corn syrup, and sugar mixture until all lumps are dissolved. 3. Eliminate the pot from heat and fold in the vanilla extract, chocolate chips, and Buncha Crunch. 4. Move the mixture into an empty Ninja CREAMI pint after refrigerating for 6 hours. 5. Fasten the lid of the pint and freeze for 24 hours. 6. After 24 hours, open the pint, fix it into the outer bowl of Ninja CREAMi along with the 'Creamerizer paddle'. 7. Fasten the lid, turn on the 'Power Button', and select the 'ICE CREAM' function. 8. Dish out the ice cream from the pint and serve chilled.

Serving Suggestions: Serve topped with graham cracker.
Variation Tip: You can also use white chocolate chips.
Nutritional Information per Serving:
Calories: 331 | Fat: 17.3g | Sat Fat: 9.8g | Carbohydrates: 44.1g | Fiber: 4.9g | Sugar: 27.2g | Protein: 4.8g

Cherry Ice Cream

⏲ **Prep: 10 minutes** ◈ **Serves: 4**

Ingredients:

1 cup full-fat coconut milk
1¼ cups frozen cherries
1 teaspoon almond extract

Preparation:

1. In a high-powered blender, add coconut milk and remaining ingredients and process until smooth. 2. Transfer the blended mixture into an empty Ninja CREAMi pint container. 3. Cover the container with storage lid and freeze for 24 hours. 4. After 24 hours, remove the lid from container and arrange into the outer bowl of Ninja CREAMi. 5. Install the "Creamerizer Paddle" onto the lid of outer bowl. 6. Then rotate the lid clockwise to lock. 7. Press "Power" button to turn on the unit. 8. Then press "ICE CREAM" button. 9. When the program is completed, turn the outer bowl and release it from the machine. 10. Transfer the ice cream into serving bowls and enjoy immediately.

Serving Suggestions: Serve with a topping of chocolate chips.
Variation Tip: You can use vanilla extract instead of almond extract.
Nutritional Information per Serving:
Calories: 145 | Fat: 12.2g | Sat Fat: 11.1g | Carbohydrates: 7.5g | Fiber: 0.8g | Sugar: 5.5g | Protein: 1.5g

Chapter 4 Ice Creams

Sea Salt Caramel Ice Cream

⏱ Prep: 10 minutes 🍽 Serves: 4

Ingredients:

1 (14-ounce) can dulce de leche
1¼ cups heavy cream
1 teaspoon sea salt flakes
1-3 tablespoons bourbon

Preparation:

1. In a large-sized bowl, place dulce de leche, cream and salt and with a hand mixer, whisk until mixture becomes thick. 2. Add in the bourbon and gently stir to blend. 3. Transfer the blended mixture into an empty Ninja CREAMi pint container. 4. Cover the container with storage lid and freeze for 24 hours. 5. After 24 hours, remove the lid from container and arrange into the outer bowl of Ninja CREAMi. 6. Install the "Creamerizer Paddle" onto the lid of outer bowl. 7. Then rotate the lid clockwise to lock. 8. Press "Power" button to turn on the unit. 9. Then press "ICE CREAM" button. 10. When the program is completed, turn the outer bowl and release it from the machine. 11. Transfer the ice cream into serving bowls and enjoy immediately.

Serving Suggestions: Serve with a garnishing of pecans.
Variation Tip: Add some milk if desired.
Nutritional Information per Serving:
Calories: 435 |Fat: 27.1g|Sat Fat: 15.3g|Carbohydrates: 47.4g|Fiber: 0g|Sugar: 39.7g|Protein: 0.8g

Coconut Ice Cream

⏱ Prep: 10 minutes 🍲 Cook: 10 minutes 🍽 Serves: 4

Ingredients:

2 tablespoons coconut, shredded
1 cup full-fat unsweetened coconut milk
2 tablespoon whipped cream
⅓ cup sugar, granulated

Preparation:

1. In a saucepan, merge together all the ingredients and simmer for 10 minutes. 2. Eliminate from heat and blitz the mixture after it is cooled down. 3. Move the mixture into an empty Ninja CREAMi pint. 4. Fasten the lid of the pint and freeze for 24 hours. 5. After 24 hours, open the pint, fix it into the outer bowl of Ninja CREAMi along with the 'Creamerizer paddle'. 6. Fasten the lid, turn on the 'Power Button', and select the 'ICE CREAM' function. 7. Dish out the ice cream from the pint and serve chilled.

Serving Suggestions: Top with caramel syrup.
Variation Tip: You can skip the cream.
Nutritional Information per Serving:
Calories: 231 | Fat: 17g | Sat Fat: 14g | Carbohydrates: 20g | Fiber: 1g | Sugar: 18g | Protein: 1.6g

Delicious Caramel Ice Cream

⏱ **Prep:** 15 minutes 🍲 **Cook:** 25 seconds ❄ **Serves:** 4

Ingredients:

1 tablespoon cream cheese
⅓ cup granulated sugar
1 teaspoon vanilla extract
½ teaspoon salt
1 cup whole milk
¾ cup heavy cream
2 tablespoons caramel dip

Preparation:

1. In a large-sized microwave-safe bowl, add the cream cheese and microwave on High for about 10 seconds. 2. Remove from the microwave and stir until smooth. 3. Add the sugar, vanilla extract and salt and with a wire whisk, beat until the mixture looks like frosting. 4. Slowly add the milk and heavy cream and whisk until blended thoroughly. 5. In a small-sized microwave-safe bowl, add the caramel dip and microwave on High for about 10-15 seconds. 6. Place the caramel dip into the bowl of milk mixture and mix well. 7. Transfer the blended mixture into an empty Ninja CREAMi pint container. 8. Cover the container with storage lid and freeze for 24 hours. 9. After 24 hours, remove the lid from container and arrange into the outer bowl of Ninja CREAMi. 10. Install the "Creamerizer Paddle" onto the lid of outer bowl. 11. Then rotate the lid clockwise to lock. 12. Press "Power" button to turn on the unit. 13. Then press "ICE CREAM" button. 14. When the program is completed, turn the outer bowl and release it from the machine. 15. Transfer the ice cream into serving bowls and enjoy immediately.

Serving Suggestions: Serve with a topping of pretzels or potato chips.
Variation Tip: You can add a sprinkle of sea salt for an extra punch of flavor.
Nutritional Information per Serving:
Calories: 218 |Fat: 11.9g|Sat Fat: 7.5g|Carbohydrates: 26.3g|Fiber: 0g|Sugar: 23.5g|Protein: 2.9g

Banana Ice Cream

⏱ **Prep:** 10 minutes ❄ **Serves:** 4

Ingredients:

1½ cups overripe bananas, peeled and sliced
3 tablespoons monk fruit sweetener
1 cup coconut cream
1 teaspoon banana extract

Preparation:

1. In a bowl, add the coconut cream and whisk until smooth. 2. Add the banana slices and with the back of a fork, lightly mash them. 3. Add in the monk fruit sweetener and banana extract and stir until blended thoroughly. 4. Transfer the blended mixture into an empty Ninja CREAMi pint container. 5. Cover the container with storage lid and freeze for 24 hours. 6. After 24 hours, remove the lid from container and arrange into the outer bowl of Ninja CREAMi. 7. Install the "Creamerizer Paddle" onto the lid of outer bowl. 8. Then rotate the lid clockwise to lock. 9. Press "Power" button to turn on the unit. 10. Then press "ICE CREAM" button. 11. When the program is completed, turn the outer bowl and release it from the machine. 12. Transfer the ice cream into serving bowls and enjoy immediately.

Serving Suggestions: Serve with a topping of caramel sauce.
Variation Tip: You can replace banana extract with vanilla extract.
Nutritional Information per Serving:
Calories: 191 |Fat: 14.5g|Sat Fat: 12.7g|Carbohydrates: 16.3g|Fiber: 2.8g|Sugar: 9g|Protein: 2g

Chapter 4 Ice Creams

Vanilla Peach Ice Cream

⏱ **Prep: 10 minutes** ≋ **Serves: 4**

Ingredients:
1 (23½-ounce) jar sliced peaches, drained
⅓ cup sweetened almond milk creamer
2 tablespoons monk fruit sweetener
½ teaspoon vanilla bean powder

Preparation:
1. In an empty Ninja CREAMi pint container, place the sliced peaches. 2. In a small-sized bowl, blend together the creamer, monk fruit sweetener and vanilla bean powder. 3. Pour the creamer mixture over the peaches. 4. Cover the container with storage lid and freeze for 24 hours. 5. After 24 hours, remove the lid from container and arrange into the outer bowl of Ninja CREAMi. 6. Install the "Creamerizer Paddle" onto the lid of outer bowl. 7. Then rotate the lid clockwise to lock. 8. Press "Power" button to turn on the unit. 9. Then press "ICE CREAM" button. 10. When the program is completed, turn the outer bowl and release it from the machine. 11. Transfer the ice cream into serving bowls and enjoy immediately.

Serving Suggestions: Serve with a garnishing of peach slices.
Variation Tip: For best result, use overripe peaches.
Nutritional Information per Serving:
Calories: 359 |Fat: 2.3g|Sat Fat: 0g|Carbohydrates: 84.5g|Fiber: 13.2g|Sugar: 84.5g|Protein: 8.1g

Banana Pineapple Rum Ice Cream

⏱ **Prep: 10 minutes** ≋ **Serves: 4**

Ingredients:
8 ounces canned pineapple chunks in juice
½ cup lite coconut cream
¼ cup maple syrup
1½ teaspoons rum extract
½ cup banana, peeled and sliced

Preparation:
1. In a large-sized bowl, add pineapple chunks, coconut cream, maple syrup and rum extract and stir until blended thoroughly. 2. Add banana slices and gently stir to blend. 3. Transfer the blended mixture into an empty Ninja CREAMi pint container. 4. Cover the container with storage lid and freeze for 24 hours. 5. After 24 hours, remove the lid from container and arrange into the outer bowl of Ninja CREAMi. 6. Install the "Creamerizer Paddle" onto the lid of outer bowl. 7. Then rotate the lid clockwise to lock. 8. Press "Power" button to turn on the unit. 9. Then press "ICE CREAM" button. 10. When the program is completed, turn the outer bowl and release it from the machine. 11. Transfer the ice cream into serving bowls and enjoy immediately.

Serving Suggestions: Serve topped with caramel sauce.
Variation Tip: You can also leave out the banana.
Nutritional Information per Serving:
Calories: 165 |Fat: 77.3g|Sat Fat: 6.4g|Carbohydrates: 26.6g|Fiber: 1.9g|Sugar: 20.6g|Protein: 1.2g

Pumpkin Brown Sugar Ice Cream

⏲ **Prep: 10 minutes** ◈ **Serves: 4**

Ingredients:

1¼ cups full-fat coconut milk, warmed and cooled
½ cup canned pumpkin puree
½ cup brown sugar, packed
1 tablespoon rum
2 teaspoons pure vanilla paste
½ teaspoon ground cinnamon
¼ teaspoon ground nutmeg
⅛ teaspoon xanthan gum

Preparation:

1. In a large-sized high-powered blender, add all of the ingredients and process until smooth. 2. Transfer the blended mixture into an empty Ninja CREAMi pint container. 3. Transfer the blended mixture into an empty Ninja CREAMi pint container. 4. Cover the container with storage lid and freeze for 24 hours. 5. After 24 hours, remove the lid from container and arrange into the outer bowl of Ninja CREAMi. 6. Install the "Creamerizer Paddle" onto the lid of outer bowl. 7. Then rotate the lid clockwise to lock. 8. Press "Power" button to turn on the unit. 9. Then press "ICE CREAM" button. 10. When the program is completed, turn the outer bowl and release it from the machine. 11. Transfer the ice cream into serving bowls and enjoy immediately.

Serving Suggestions: Serve topped with cream.
Variation Tip: Don't use pumpkin pie mix instead of pumpkin puree.
Nutritional Information per Serving:
Calories: 234 |Fat: 15.1g|Sat Fat: 13.8g|Carbohydrates: 23.3g|Fiber: 1.2g|Sugar: 19.9g|Protein: 1.6g

Mocha Ice Cream

⏲ **Prep: 10 minutes** ◈ **Serves: 4**

Ingredients:

½ cup mocha cappuccino mix
1¾ cups coconut cream
3 tablespoons agave nectar

Preparation:

1. In a bowl, add all of the ingredients and beat until well combined. 2. Transfer the mixture into an empty Ninja CREAMi pint container. 3. Cover the container with storage lid and freeze for 24 hours. 4. After 24 hours, remove the lid from container and arrange into the Outer Bowl of Ninja CREAMi. 5. Install the Creamerizer Paddle onto the lid of Outer Bowl. 6. Then rotate the lid clockwise to lock. 7. Press Power button to turn on the unit. 8. Then press Ice Cream button. 9. When the program is completed, turn the Outer Bowl and release it from the machine. 10. Transfer the ice cream into serving bowls and serve immediately.

Serving Suggestions: Serve with the garnishing of almond slices.
Variation Tip: You can use fresh cream instead of coconut cream.
Nutritional Information per Serving:
Calories: 297 | Fat: 25.4g|Sat Fat: 22.3g|Carbohydrates: 19.2g|Fiber: 3.1g|Sugar: 15.4g|Protein: 2.5g

Pear Ice Cream

⏱ Prep: 15 minutes 🍳 Cook: 15 minutes 🍽 Serves: 4

Ingredients:

1 (14-ounce) can full-fat unsweetened coconut milk
3 medium pears, peeled, cored and cut into 1-inch pieces
½ cup sugar, granulated

Preparation:

1. In a saucepan, merge together all the ingredients and stir well. 2. Thoroughly boil and switch the heat to low, so that it simmers for 10 minutes. 3. Eliminate from the heat and blitz the mixture after it is cooled down. 4. Move the mixture into an empty Ninja CREAMI pint. 5. Fasten the lid of the pint and freeze for 24 hours. 6. After 24 hours, open the pint, fix it into the outer bowl of Ninja CREAMi along with the 'Creamerizer paddle'. 7. Fasten the lid, turn on the 'Power Button', and select the 'ICE CREAM' function. 8. Dish out the ice cream from the pint and serve chilled.

Serving Suggestions: Serve topped with whipped cream and caramel syrup.
Variation Tip: It is best to use ripe pears.
Nutritional Information per Serving:

Calories: 368 | Fat: 18.5g | Sat Fat: 168g | Carbohydrates: 51.9g | Fiber: 4.9g | Sugar: 41.8g | Protein: 2.1g

Blackberry Ice Cream

⏱ Prep: 30 minutes 🍳 Cook: 5 minutes 🍽 Serves: 2

Ingredients:

½ pint fresh blackberries
¼ cup white sugar
½ teaspoon lemon zest
1 cup heavy cream
⅓ cup whole milk
1 teaspoon vanilla extract

Preparation:

1. Puree the blackberries, sugar, and lemon zest in a blender. 2. Put the purée in a mixing bowl after straining the seeds through a fine-mesh sieve. 3. Combine the cream, milk, and vanilla extract in a mixing bowl. Mix for about 30 seconds or until the mixture is whipped. Add to the purée and mix well. 4. Pour the mixture into an empty ninja CREAMi Pint container and freeze for 24 hours. 5. After 24 hours, remove the Pint from the freezer. Remove the lid. 6. Place the Ninja CREAMi Pint into the outer bowl. Place the outer bowl with the Pint in it into the ninja CREAMi machine and turn until the outer bowl locks into place. Push the ICE CREAM button. 7. Once the ICE CREAM function has ended, turn the outer bowl and release it from the ninja CREAMi machine.

Serving Suggestion: Serve immediately.
Variation Tip: Sprinkle cinnamon over it if you like.
Nutritional Information per Serving:

Calories 560 | Protein 4.4g | Carbohydrate 37g | Dietary Fiber 3.5g | Sugar 30g | Fat 45g | Sodium 58mg

Chapter 5 Ice Cream Mix-In

Pretzel Ice Cream ………………………………………………… 46

Lemon Oreo Ice Cream ………………………………………… 46

Peanut and Grape Jelly Ice Cream …………………………… 47

Chocolate Walnut Ice cream …………………………………… 47

Lavender and Chocolate Wafer Ice Cream ………………… 48

Apple and Graham Crackers Ice Cream …………………… 48

Banana Oreo Ice Cream ………………………………………… 49

Mint Chocolate Cookies Ice Cream ………………………… 49

Blueberry & Graham Cracker Ice Cream …………………… 50

Chocolate Spinach Ice Cream ………………………………… 50

Cheese Pecan Raspberry Ice Cream ………………………… 51

Peanut Butter Chips Ice Cream ……………………………… 51

Chocolate Chips Cherry Ice Cream ………………………… 52

Chocolate Sea Salt Ice Cream………………………………… 52

Pretzel Ice Cream

⏱ **Prep: 10 minutes**　🍳 **Cook: 1 minute**　🍽 **Serves: 2**

Ingredients:

½ tablespoon cream cheese, softened
⅓ cup cream
1 tablespoon vanilla extract
3 tablespoons sugar
½ cup whole milk

Mix-Ins:
½ tablespoon mini pretzels

Preparation:

1. In a large microwave-safe bowl, microwave the cream cheese for 12 seconds. 2. In a bowl, merge together the sugar and vanilla extract. Let it rest for 30 minutes. 3. Fold in the heavy cream and milk and whisk well. 4. Move the mixture into an empty Ninja CREAMI pint. 5. Fasten the lid of the pint and freeze for 24 hours. 6. After 24 hours, open the pint, fix it into the outer bowl of Ninja CREAMi along with the 'Creamerizer paddle'. 7. Fasten the lid, turn on the 'Power Button', and select the 'ICE CREAM' function. 8. Now, make a wide hole in the center that reaches the bottom of the pint. 9. Put the mini pretzels in the hole and select the 'MIX-IN' function. 10. Dish out the ice cream from the pint and serve chilled.

Serving Suggestions: Top with caramel sauce and more pretzels.
Variation Tip: You can use heavy cream instead of cream cheese.
Nutritional Information per Serving:
Calories: 189 | Fat: 11g | Sat Fat: 6.9g | Carbohydrates: 20g | Fiber: 0g | Sugar: 20g | Protein: 2.7g

Lemon Oreo Ice Cream

⏱ **Prep: 10 minutes**　🍳 **Cook: 10 seconds**　🍽 **Serves: 4**

Ingredients:

1 tablespoon cream cheese, softened
⅓ cup granulated sugar
1 teaspoon lemon extract
1 cup whole milk
¾ cup heavy cream
3-4 Oreo cookies, crushed

Preparation:

1. In a large-sized microwave-safe bowl, add the cream cheese and microwave on High for about 10 seconds. 2. Remove from the microwave and stir until smooth. 3. Add the sugar and lemon extract and with a wire whisk, whisk until the mixture looks like frosting. 4. Slowly add the milk and heavy cream and whisk until blended thoroughly. 5. Transfer the blended mixture into an empty Ninja CREAMi pint container. 6. Cover the container with storage lid and freeze for 24 hours. 7. After 24 hours, remove the lid from container and arrange into the outer bowl of Ninja CREAMi. 8. Install the "Creamerizer Paddle" onto the lid of outer bowl. 9. Then rotate the lid clockwise to lock. 10. Press "Power" button to turn on the unit. 11. Then press "ICE CREAM" button. 12. When the program is completed, with a spoon, create a 1½-inch wide hole in the center that reaches the bottom of the pint container. 13. Add the crushed Oreos in the hole and press "MIX-IN" button. 14. When the program is completed, turn the outer bowl and release it from the machine. 15. Transfer the ice cream into serving bowls and enjoy immediately.

Serving Suggestions: Serve with a topping of whipped cream.
Variation Tip: Use full-fat cream cheese.
Nutritional Information per Serving:
Calories: 223 | Fat: 12.6g | Sat Fat: 7.2g | Carbohydrates: 25.6g | Fiber: 0.2g | Sugar: 23.1g | Protein: 3g

Chapter 5 Ice Cream Mix-In

Peanut and Grape Jelly Ice Cream

⏰ Prep: 25 minutes 🍲 Cook: 3 minutes 🍨 Serves: 4

Ingredients:
4 large egg yolks
⅓ cup heavy cream
¼ cup smooth peanut butter
¼ cup honey roasted peanuts, chopped
3 tablespoons sugar, granulated
1 cup whole milk
3 tablespoons grape jelly

Preparation:
1. In a small saucepan, merge together the egg yolks and sugar. 2. Fold in the heavy cream, milk, peanut butter, and grape jelly. 3. Cook till it reaches a temperature of 175°F, stirring constantly. 4. Eliminate from the heat and permit it to cool down. 5. Move the mixture into an empty Ninja CREAMI pint. 6. Fasten the lid of the pint and freeze for 24 hours. 7. After 24 hours, open the pint, fix it into the outer bowl of Ninja CREAMi along with the 'Creamerizer paddle'. 8. Fasten the lid, turn on the 'Power Button', and select the 'ICE CREAM' function. 9. Now, make a wide hole in the center that reaches the bottom of the pint. 10. Put the honey roasted peanuts in the hole and select the 'MIX-IN' function. 11. Dish out the ice cream from the pint and serve chilled.

Serving Suggestions: Serve topped with jelly.
Variation Tip: You can use any desired flavor of jelly.
Nutritional Information per Serving:
Calories: 340 | Fat: 22g | Sat Fat: 7g | Carbohydrates: 26g | Fiber: 1g | Sugar: 20g | Protein: 11g

Chocolate Walnut Ice cream

⏰ Prep: 10 minutes 🍨 Serves: 6

Ingredients:
1 cup whole milk
⅓ cup sugar, granulated
2 tablespoons cocoa powder
½ cup walnuts, chopped
¾ cup heavy cream
2 tablespoons mini chocolate chips
½ cup brownies, chopped

Preparation:
1. In a blender, blitz all the ingredients except walnuts until smooth. 2. Move the mixture into an empty Ninja CREAMI pint. 3. Fasten the lid of the pint and freeze for 24 hours. 4. After 24 hours, open the pint, fix it into the outer bowl of Ninja CREAMi along with the 'Creamerizer paddle'. 5. Fasten the lid, turn on the 'Power Button', and select the 'ICE CREAM' function. 6. Now, make a wide hole in the center that reaches the bottom of the pint. 7. Put the walnuts in the hole and select the 'MIX-IN' function. 8. Dish out the ice cream from the pint and serve chilled.

Serving Suggestions: Serve with chocolate sauce on top.
Variation Tip: You can also add cranberries.
Nutritional Information per Serving:
Calories: 269 | Fat: 16.7g | Sat Fat: 5.8g | Carbohydrates: 28.6g | Fiber: 1.3g | Sugar: 13.5g | Protein: 5.4g

Lavender and Chocolate Wafer Ice Cream

⏰ **Prep: 15 minutes**　🍲 **Cook: 10 minutes**　🍽 **Serves: 4**

Ingredients:

¾ cup heavy cream
⅛ teaspoon salt
¾ cup whole milk
4 drops purple food coloring
1 tablespoon dried culinary lavender
½ cup condensed milk, sweetened
⅓ cup chocolate wafer cookies, crushed

Preparation:

1. In a saucepan, merge together heavy cream, lavender, and salt. 2. Cook for about 10 minutes, stirring constantly. 3. Eliminate from the heat and strain the cream mixture in a large bowl. 4. Eliminate the lavender leaves and fold in the milk, condensed milk and purple food coloring. 5. Move the mixture into an empty Ninja CREAMI pint. 6. Fasten the lid of the pint and freeze for 24 hours. 7. After 24 hours, open the pint, fix it into the outer bowl of Ninja CREAMi along with the 'Creamerizer paddle'. 8. Fasten the lid, turn on the 'Power Button', and select the 'ICE CREAM' function. 9. Now, make a wide hole in the center that reaches the bottom of the pint. 10. Put the crushed cookies in the hole and select the 'MIX-IN' function. 11. Dish out the ice cream from the pint and serve chilled.

Serving Suggestions: Serve topped chocolate chunks.
Variation Tip: You can use any flavor of wafer cookies.
Nutritional Information per Serving:
Calories: 229 | Fat: 13.2g | Sat Fat: 8.1g | Carbohydrates: 23.5g | Fiber: 0g | Sugar: 23.2g | Protein: 5g

Apple and Graham Crackers Ice Cream

⏰ **Prep: 10 minutes**　🍲 **Cook: 10 seconds**　🍽 **Serves: 4**

Ingredients:

1 tablespoon cream cheese, softened
2 tablespoons brown sugar
¾ teaspoon apple pie spice
½ cup heavy cream
¼ cup whole milk
1 cup canned apple pie filling
¼-½ cup graham crackers, chopped

Preparation:

1. In a large-sized microwave-safe bowl, add the cream cheese and microwave on High for about 10 seconds. 2. Remove from the microwave and stir until smooth. 3. Add the brown sugar and apple pie spice and with a wire whisk, whisk until the mixture looks like frosting. 4. In a separate large-sized bowl, add heavy cream, milk, and apple pie filling and with an immersion blender, whip until apples are chopped into small pieces. 5. Gradually add the milk mixture into the bowl of sugar mixture and whisk until blended thoroughly. 6. Transfer the blended mixture into an empty Ninja CREAMi pint container. 7. Place the container into an ice bath to cool. 8. After cooling, cover the container with the storage lid and freeze for 24 hours. 9. After 24 hours, remove the lid from container and arrange into the outer bowl of Ninja CREAMi. 10. Install the "Creamerizer Paddle" onto the lid of outer bowl. 11. Then rotate the lid clockwise to lock. 12. Press "Power" button to turn on the unit. 13. Then press "ICE CREAM" button. 14. When the program is completed, with a spoon, create a 1½-inch wide hole in the center that reaches the bottom of the pint container. 15. Add the chopped graham crackers in the hole and press "MIX-IN" button. 16. When the program is completed, turn the outer bowl and release it from the machine. 17. Transfer the ice cream into serving bowls and enjoy immediately.

Serving Suggestions: Serve with a side of fresh apple slices.
Variation Tip: Brown sugar can be replaced with white sugar too.
Nutritional Information per Serving:
Calories: 201 | Fat: 7.5g | Sat Fat: 4.4g | Carbohydrates: 31.8g | Fiber: 0.9g | Sugar: 22g | Protein: 4g

Banana Oreo Ice Cream

⏲ **Prep: 10 minutes** ❖ **Serves: 4**

Ingredients:

½ cup coconut cream
½ cup oat milk
¼ cup dry instant banana pudding mix
2 tablespoons granulated sugar
1 tablespoon cream cheese, softened
1½ teaspoons vanilla extract
⅔ cup banana, peeled and sliced
3 Oreo cookies, crushed

Preparation:

1. In a large-sized bowl, add coconut cream, oat milk, pudding mix, sugar, cream cheese and vanilla extract and with a wire whisk, whisk until the mixture looks like frosting. 2. Add banana slices and stir to blend. 3. Transfer the blended mixture into an empty Ninja CREAMi pint container. 4. Place the container into an ice bath to cool. 5. After cooling, cover the container with the storage lid and freeze for 24 hours. 6. After 24 hours, remove the lid from container and arrange into the outer bowl of Ninja CREAMi. 7. Install the "Creamerizer Paddle" onto the lid of outer bowl. 8. Then rotate the lid clockwise to lock. 9. Press "Power" button to turn on the unit. 10. Then press "ICE CREAM" button. 11. When the program is completed, with a spoon, create a 1½-inch wide hole in the center that reaches the bottom of the pint container. 12. Add the crushed Oreos in the hole and press "MIX-IN" button. 13. When the program is completed, turn the outer bowl and release it from the machine. 14. Transfer the ice cream into serving bowls and enjoy immediately.

Serving Suggestions: Serve with a garnishing of extra cookies.
Variation Tip: You can use cookies of your choice.
Nutritional Information per Serving:
Calories: 171 |Fat: 10g|Sat Fat: 7.3g|Carbohydrates: 19.1g|Fiber: 1.1g|Sugar: 12.6g|Protein: 2.2g

Mint Chocolate Cookies Ice Cream

⏲ **Prep: 15 minutes** ❖ **Serves: 4**

Ingredients:

¾ cup coconut cream
¼ cup monk fruit sweetener with Erythritol
2 tablespoons agave nectar
½ teaspoon mint extract
5-6 drops green food coloring
1 cup oat milk
3 chocolate sandwich cookies, quartered

Preparation:

1. In a large bowl, add the coconut cream and beat until smooth. 2. Add the sweetener, agave nectar, mint extract and food coloring and beat until sweetener is dissolved. 3. Add the oat milk and beat until well combined. 4. Transfer the mixture into an empty Ninja CREAMi pint container. 5. Cover the container with storage lid and freeze for 24 hours. 6. After 24 hours, remove the lid from container and arrange into the Outer Bowl of Ninja CREAMi. 7. Install the Creamerizer Paddle onto the lid of Outer Bowl. 8. Then rotate the lid clockwise to lock. 9. Press Power button to turn on the unit. 10. Then press Lite Ice Cream button. 11. When the program is completed, with a spoon, create a 1½-inch wide hole in the center that reaches the bottom of the pint container. 12. Add the cookie pieces into the hole and press Mix-In button. 13. When the program is completed, turn the Outer Bowl and release it from the machine. 14. Transfer the ice cream into serving bowls and serve immediately.

Serving Suggestions: Serve with the garnishing of chocolate chunks.
Variation Tip: make sure to use mint extract.
Nutritional Information per Serving:
Calories: 201 | Fat: 12.8g|Sat Fat: 9.8g|Carbohydrates: 21.9g|Fiber: 2.2g|Sugar: 16.8g|Protein: 2.4g

Chapter 5 Ice Cream Mix-In | 49

Blueberry & Graham Cracker Ice Cream

⏲ **Prep: 15 minutes**   🍳 **Cook: 5 minutes**   🍽 **Serves: 4**

Ingredients:

- 1 cup fresh blueberries
- ¼ cup plus 1 teaspoon sugar, divided
- ½ teaspoon lemon juice
- 1 cup milk
- ½ cup half-and-half
- 2 tablespoons instant vanilla pudding mix
- 1 graham cracker, crushed
- 1 teaspoon butter, melted
- ¼ teaspoon ground cinnamon

Preparation:

1. **For pie filling:** in a small-sized saucepan, add the blueberries, ¼ cup of sugar, and lemon juice over medium heat and cook for about 5 minutes or until the sugar is dissolved, stirring continuously. 2. Remove the pan of filling from heat and set aside to cool. 3. In an empty Ninja CREAMi pint container, place milk, half-and-half and pudding mix and with a wire whisk, beat until blended thoroughly. 4. Add the filling mixture and mix well. 5. Cover the container with storage lid and freeze for 24 hours. 6. After 24 hours, remove the lid from container and arrange into the outer bowl of Ninja CREAMi. 7. Install the "Creamerizer Paddle" onto the lid of outer bowl. 8. Then rotate the lid clockwise to lock. 9. Press "Power" button to turn on the unit. 10. Then press "ICE CREAM" button. 11. Meanwhile, in a medium-sized bowl, add graham cracker, butter, remaining sugar and cinnamon and mix well. 12. When the program is completed, with a spoon, create a 1½-inch wide hole in the center that reaches the bottom of the pint container. 13. Add the cracker mixture in the hole and press "MIX-IN" button. 14. When the program is completed, turn the outer bowl and release it from the machine. 15. Transfer the ice cream into serving bowls and enjoy immediately.

Serving Suggestions: Serve with a garnishing of fresh blueberries.
Variation Tip: You can use crushed pie crust instead of graham cracker.
Nutritional Information per Serving:
Calories: 177 |Fat: 7.2g |Sat Fat: 4.1g|Carbohydrates: 26.4g |Fiber: 1.1g |Sugar: 22.1g |Protein: 3.7g

Chocolate Spinach Ice Cream

⏲ **Prep: 15 minutes**   🍽 **Serves: 4**

Ingredients:

- ½ cup frozen spinach, thawed and squeezed dry
- 1 cup whole milk
- ½ cup granulated sugar
- 1 teaspoon mint extract
- 3-5 drops green food coloring
- ⅓ cup heavy cream
- ¼ cup chocolate chunks, chopped
- ¼ cup brownie, cut into 1-inch pieces

Preparation:

1. In a high-speed blender, add the spinach, milk, sugar, mint extract and food coloring and pulse until mixture smooth. 2. Transfer the mixture into an empty Ninja CREAMi pint container. 3. Add the heavy cream and stir until well combined. 4. Cover the container with storage lid and freeze for 24 hours. 5. After 24 hours, remove the lid from container and arrange into the Outer Bowl of Ninja CREAMi. 6. Install the Creamerizer Paddle onto the lid of Outer Bowl. 7. Then rotate the lid clockwise to lock. 8. Press Power button to turn on the unit. 9. Then press Ice Cream button. 10. When the program is completed, with a spoon, create a 1½-inch wide hole in the center that reaches the bottom of the pint container. 11. Add the chocolate chunks and brownie pieces into the hole and press Mix-In button. 12. When the program is completed, turn the Outer Bowl and release it from the machine. 13. Transfer the ice cream into serving bowls and serve immediately.

Serving Suggestions: Serve with the garnishing of chocolate shaving.
Variation Tip: Make sure to squeeze the spinach completely.
Nutritional Information per Serving:
Calories: 243 | Fat: 10.1g|Sat Fat: 6g|Carbohydrates: 36.7g|Fiber: 0.4g|Sugar: 33.7g|Protein: 3.4g

Chapter 5 Ice Cream Mix-In

Cheese Pecan Raspberry Ice Cream

⏲ **Prep: 10 minutes** 🍳 **Cook: 5 minutes** 🍽 **Serves: 4**

Ingredients:

1 cup heavy cream
½ cup whole milk
¼ cup maple syrup
2 ounces ricotta cheese
2 tablespoons raspberry jam
2 tablespoons lime curd
¼ cup pecans, chopped

Preparation:

1. In a small-sized saucepan, put in cream, milk, and maple syrup on burner at around medium heat and cook until heated through, stirring continuously. 2. Add in the ricotta cheese and blend to incorporate thoroughly. 3. Transfer the blended mixture into an empty Ninja CREAMi pint container. 4. Place the container into an ice bath to cool. 5. After cooling, cover the container with the storage lid and freeze for 24 hours. 6. After 24 hours, take off the lid from container and arrange into the outer bowl of Ninja CREAMi. 7. Install the "Creamerizer Paddle" onto the lid of outer bowl. 8. Then rotate the lid clockwise to lock. 9. Press "Power" button to turn on the unit. 10. Then press "ICE CREAM" button. 11. When the program is completed, with a spoon, create a 1½-inch wide hole in the center that reaches the bottom of the pint container. 12. Put in jam, lime curd and pecans in the hole and press "MIX-IN" button. 13. When the program is completed, turn the outer bowl and release it from the machine. 14. Transfer the ice cream into serving bowls and enjoy immediately.

Serving Suggestions: Serve alongside fresh raspberries.
Variation Tip: Feel free to use jam of your choice.
Nutritional Information per Serving:
Calories: 356 |Fat: 39.3g|Sat Fat: 10.3g|Carbohydrates: 27.4g|Fiber: 1.7g|Sugar: 27.4g|Protein: 5.4g

Peanut Butter Chips Ice Cream

⏲ **Prep: 10 minutes** 🍳 **Cook: 10 seconds** 🍽 **Serves: 4**

Ingredients:

1 tablespoon cream cheese
⅓ cup granulated sugar
1 teaspoon vanilla extract
¾ cup heavy cream
1 cup whole milk
¼ cup peanut butter chips

Preparation:

1. In a large-sized, microwave-safe bowl, put in cream cheese and microwave for 10 seconds. 2. Put in sugar and vanilla extract and whisk to form a frosting mixture. 3. Slowly put in the heavy cream and milk and whisk to incorporate thoroughly. 4. Transfer the blended mixture into an empty Ninja CREAMi pint container. 5. Cover the container with the storage lid and freeze for 24 hours. 6. After 24 hours, take off the lid from container and arrange into the outer bowl of Ninja CREAMi. 7. Install the "Creamerizer Paddle" onto the lid of outer bowl. 8. Then rotate the lid clockwise to lock. 9. Press "Power" button to turn on the unit. 10. Then press "ICE CREAM" button. 11. When the program is completed, with a spoon, create a 1½-inch wide hole in the center that reaches the bottom of the pint container. 12. Add peanut butter chips in the hole and press "MIX-IN" button. 13. When the program is completed, turn the outer bowl and release it from the machine. 14. Transfer the ice cream into serving bowls and enjoy immediately.

Serving Suggestions: This ice cream will go greatly with fruit crumbles.
Variation Tip: Use full-fat cream cheese.
Nutritional Information per Serving:
Calories: 259 |Fat: 15.2g|Sat Fat: 9.9g|Carbohydrates: 29.3g|Fiber: 0g|Sugar: 29g|Protein: 2.6g

Chocolate Chips Cherry Ice Cream

⏱ Prep: 15 minutes 🍴 Serves: 4

Ingredients:

½ cup frozen cherries, thawed and squeezed
½ cup granulated sugar
1 cup whole milk
½ teaspoon vanilla extract
½ teaspoon strawberry extract
⅓ cup heavy cream
⅓ cup chocolate chips

Preparation:

1. In a high-powered blender, put in cherries and remaining ingredients except for chocolate chips and process to form a smooth mixture. 2. Transfer the blended mixture into an empty Ninja CREAMi pint container. 3. Put in heavy cream and blend to incorporate. 4. Cover the container with the storage lid and freeze for 24 hours. 5. After 24 hours, take off the lid from container and arrange into the outer bowl of Ninja CREAMi. 6. Install the "Creamerizer Paddle" onto the lid of outer bowl. 7. Then rotate the lid clockwise to lock. 8. Press "Power" button to turn on the unit. 9. Then press "ICE CREAM" button. 10. When the program is completed, with a spoon, create a 1½-inch wide hole in the center that reaches the bottom of the pint container. 11. Add chocolate chips in the hole and press "MIX-IN" button. 12. When the program is completed, turn the outer bowl and release it from the machine. 13. Transfer the ice cream into serving bowls and enjoy immediately.

Serving Suggestions: Serve with a garnishing of chocolate chips.
Variation Tip: You can use more vanilla extract instead of strawberry extract.
Nutritional Information per Serving:
Calories: 250 |Fat: 9.9g|Sat Fat: 6.4g|Carbohydrates: 38.6g|Fiber: 0.8g|Sugar: 37.3g|Protein: 3.4g

Chocolate Sea Salt Ice Cream

⏱ Prep: 15 minutes 🍳 Cook: 7 minutes 🍴 Serves: 4

Ingredients:

2 cups whole milk
½ cup sugar
1 teaspoon vanilla extract
Pinch of sea salt
1-ounce chocolate chips
2 teaspoons butter

Preparation:

1. In a medium saucepan, put in milk and sugar and whisk to incorporate. 2. Place saucepan on burner at around medium heat and cook for around 3-5 minutes, stirring continuously. 3. Take off the pan of milk mixture from burner and whisk in vanilla extract and salt. 4. Transfer the blended mixture into an empty Ninja CREAMi pint container. 5. Place the container into an ice bath to cool. 6. After cooling, cover the container with the storage lid and freeze for 24 hours. 7. After 24 hours, take off the lid from container and arrange into the outer bowl of Ninja CREAMi. 8. Install the "Creamerizer Paddle" onto the lid of outer bowl. 9. Then rotate the lid clockwise to lock. 10. Press "Power" button to turn on the unit. 11. Then press "ICE CREAM" button. 12. Meanwhile, in a medium-sized microwave-safe bowl, put in chocolate chips and butter and microwave on high for around 2 minutes, stirring after every 20 seconds. 13. Take off the bowl from microwave and blend until smooth. 14. Let the chocolate mixture to cool thoroughly. 15. When the program is completed, with a spoon, create a 1½-inch wide hole in the center that reaches the bottom of the pint container. 16. Add chocolate mixture in the hole and press "MIX-IN" button. 17. When the program is completed, turn the outer bowl and release it from the machine. 18. Transfer the ice cream into serving bowls and enjoy immediately.

Serving Suggestions: Serve with a topping of whipped cream.
Variation Tip: Use semi-sweet chocolate chips.
Nutritional Information per Serving:
Calories: 225 |Fat: 8g|Sat Fat: 5g|Carbohydrates: 34.9g|Fiber: 0.2g|Sugar: 35.2g|Protein: 4.5g

Chapter 6 Gelato

Maple Gelato 54

Chocolate Peanut Gelato.................................. 54

Sugar Cookies Gelato 55

Sweet Coffee Gelato 55

Cheese Mixed Berries Gelato 56

Blueberry and Graham Crackers Gelato 57

Butternut Squash and Banana Gelato 58

Red Velvet Cream Cheese Cocoa Gelato 59

Vanilla Peanut Butter Cookie Gelato 60

Flavorful Pumpkin Gelato 61

Carrot Gelato 62

Sweet Potato Banana Gelato 63

Flavorful Cream Cheese Cacao Gelato 64

Caramel Honey Hazelnut Gelato 65

Maple Gelato

⏰ **Prep: 10 minutes**   🍲 **Cook: 3 minutes**   🍽 **Serves: 4**

Ingredients:
4 large egg yolks
½ cup plus 1 tablespoon light brown sugar
1 tablespoon maple syrup
1 teaspoon maple extract
1 cup whole milk
⅓ cup heavy cream

Preparation:
1. In a small-sized saucepan, add the egg yolks, brown sugar, maple syrup and maple extract and whisk until blended thoroughly. 2. Add the milk and heavy cream and whisk until blended thoroughly. 3. Place the saucepan of milk mixture over medium heat and cook for about 2-3 minutes, stirring continuously. 4. Remove the saucepan of milk mixture from heat and through a fine-mesh strainer, strain the mixture into an empty Ninja CREAMi pint container. 5. Place the container into an ice bath to cool. 6. After cooling, cover the container with the storage lid and freeze for 24 hours. 7. After 24 hours, remove the lid from container and arrange into the outer bowl of Ninja CREAMi. 8. Install the "Creamerizer Paddle" onto the lid of outer bowl. 9. Then rotate the lid clockwise to lock. 10. Press "Power" button to turn on the unit. 11. Then press "GELATO" button. 12. When the program is completed, turn the outer bowl and release it from the machine. 13. Transfer the gelato into serving bowls and serve immediately.
Serving Suggestions: Enjoy vanilla gelato alongside a hot brownie.
Variation Tip: Look for dairy with naturally high protein content.
Nutritional Information per Serving:
Calories: 218 |Fat: 10.2g|Sat Fat: 3.1g|Carbohydrates: 27g|Fiber: 0g|Sugar: 26.1g|Protein: 4.9g

Chocolate Peanut Gelato

⏰ **Prep: 10 minutes**   🍲 **Cook: 9 minutes**   🍽 **Serves: 4**

Ingredients:
1½ cups unsweetened coconut milk
6 tablespoons sugar
1 tablespoon cornstarch
3 tablespoons peanut butter
3 dark chocolate peanut butter cups, cut each into 8 pieces
2 tablespoons peanuts, chopped

Preparation:
1. In a small-sized saucepan, add the coconut milk, sugar, and cornstarch and mix well. 2. Place the saucepan over medium heat and bring to a boil, whisking continuously. 3. Now, adjust the heat to low and simmer for about 3-4 minutes. 4. Remove the pan of milk mixture from heat and stir in the peanut butter. 5. Transfer the mixture into an empty Ninja CREAMi pint container. 6. Place the container into an ice bath to cool. 7. After cooling, cover the container with the storage lid and freeze for 24 hours. 8. After 24 hours, remove the lid from container and arrange into the outer bowl of Ninja CREAMi. 9. Install the "Creamerizer Paddle" onto the lid of outer bowl. 10. Then rotate the lid clockwise to lock. 11. Press "Power" button to turn on the unit. 12. Then press "GELATO" button. 13. When the program is completed, with a spoon, create a 1½-inch wide hole in the center that reaches the bottom of the pint container. 14. Add the peanut butter cup pieces and peanuts into the hole and press "MIX-IN" button. 15. When the program is completed, turn the outer bowl and release it from the machine. 16. Transfer the gelato into serving bowls and serve immediately.
Serving Suggestions: Serve with a topping of chopped peanuts.
Variation Tip: Use unsalted peanuts.
Nutritional Information per Serving:
Calories: 426 |Fat: 29.7g|Sat Fat: 17.3g|Carbohydrates: 34.2g|Fiber: 1.1g|Sugar: 29.1g|Protein: 6.8g

Sugar Cookies Gelato

⏰ **Prep: 10 minutes**   🍳 **Cook: 5 minutes**   🍽 **Serves: 4**

Ingredients:

1 cup whole milk
¾ cup heavy cream
⅓ cup granulated sugar
¼ cup sugar cookie mix
2 egg yolks
1 teaspoon vanilla extract

Preparation:

1. In a medium-sized saucepan, put in milk and remaining ingredients on burner at around medium heat and cook for around 5 minutes, whisking constantly. 2. Through a fine-mesh strainer, strain the blended mixture into an empty Ninja CREAMi pint container. 3. Transfer the blended mixture into a Ninja Creami pint container, making sure not to exceed the maximum fill line. 4. Place the container into an ice bath to cool. 5. After cooling, cover the container with the storage lid and freeze for 24 hours. 6. After 24 hours, take off the lid from container and arrange into the outer bowl of Ninja CREAMi. 7. Install the "Creamerizer Paddle" onto the lid of outer bowl. 8. Then rotate the lid clockwise to lock. 9. Press "Power" button to turn on the unit. 10. Then press "GELATO" button. 11. When the program is completed, turn the outer bowl and release it from the machine. 12. Transfer the gelato into serving bowls and enjoy immediately.

Serving Suggestions: Serve with a garnishing of rainbow sprinkles.
Variation Tip: Don't use low-fat milk.
Nutritional Information per Serving:
Calories: 243 |Fat: 13.4g|Sat Fat: 7.3g|Carbohydrates: 27.8g|Fiber: 0g|Sugar: 24.1g|Protein: 4.1g

Sweet Coffee Gelato

Prep: 10 minutes   **Cook: 5 minutes**   ⏰ **Serves: 4**

Ingredients:

4 egg yolks
⅓ cup honey
1¾ cups whole milk
2 tablespoons coffee powder

Preparation:

1. In a medium-sized saucepan, put in egg yolks and remaining ingredients on burner at around medium heat and cook for around 3-5 minutes, stirring continuously. 2. Through a fine-mesh strainer, strain the mixture into an empty Ninja CREAMi pint container. 3. Place the container into an ice bath to cool. 4. After cooling, cover the container with the storage lid and freeze for 24 hours. 5. After 24 hours, take off the lid from container and arrange into the outer bowl of Ninja CREAMi. 6. Install the "Creamerizer Paddle" onto the lid of outer bowl. 7. Then rotate the lid clockwise to lock. 8. Press "Power" button to turn on the unit. 9. Then press "GELATO" button. 10. When the program is completed, turn the outer bowl and release it from the machine. 11. Transfer the gelato into serving bowls and serve immediately.

Serving Suggestions: Serve with a topping of crumbled chocolate.
Variation Tip: You can use espresso powder in this recipe.
Nutritional Information per Serving:
Calories: 339 |Fat: 26.1g|Sat Fat: 21.2g|Carbohydrates: 23g|Fiber: 0.8g|Sugar: 17.5g|Protein: 5g

Cheese Mixed Berries Gelato

⏰ **Prep: 10 minutes** 🍲 **Cook: 3 minutes** ♦ **Serves: 4**

Ingredients:
3 large egg yolks
½ cup plus 2 tablespoons granulated sugar, divided
1 tablespoon light corn syrup
½ cup mascarpone
¾ cup whole milk
¼ cup heavy cream
½ teaspoon vanilla extract
1 cup frozen mixed berries

Preparation:
1. In a small-sized saucepan, add the egg yolks, ½ cup of sugar and corn syrup and whisk until blended thoroughly. 2. Add the mascarpone, milk, heavy cream and vanilla extract and whisk until blended thoroughly. 3. Place the saucepan over medium heat and cook for about 2-3 minutes, stirring continuously. 4. Remove the saucepan of milk mixture from heat and through a fine-mesh strainer, strain the mixture into an empty Ninja CREAMi pint container. 5. Place the container into an ice bath to cool. 6. After cooling, cover the container with the storage lid and freeze for 24 hours. 7. Meanwhile, in a small-sized saucepan, add the mixed berries and remaining sugar over medium heat and cook for about 8 minutes, stirring occasionally and mashing to form a thick jam. 8. Remove the saucepan of berry mixture from heat and transfer the jam into a bowl. 9. Refrigerate the frozen mixed berries until using. 10. After 24 hours, remove the lid from container and arrange the container into the outer bowl of Ninja CREAMi. 11. Install the "Creamerizer Paddle" onto the lid of outer bowl. 12. Then rotate the lid clockwise to lock. 13. Press "Power" button to turn on the unit. 14. Then press "GELATO" button. 15. When the program is completed, with a spoon, create a 1½-inch wide hole in the center that reaches the bottom of the pint container. 16. Add the mixed berries into the hole and press "MIX-IN" button. 17. When the program is completed, turn the outer bowl and release it from the machine. 18. Transfer the gelato into serving bowls and serve immediately.

Serving Suggestions: Serve with a garnishing of fresh mint.
Variation Tip: Feel free to use light molasses instead of corn syrup.
Nutritional Information per Serving:
Calories: 295 |Fat: 11.8g|Sat Fat: 2.9g|Carbohydrates: 41.6g|Fiber: 1.3g|Sugar: 36.4g|Protein: 7.4g

Blueberry and Graham Crackers Gelato

⏱ **Prep: 10 minutes**   🍲 **Cook: 3 minutes**   ❄ **Serves: 4**

Ingredients:

4 large egg yolks
3 tablespoons granulated sugar
3 tablespoons wild blueberry preserves
1 teaspoon vanilla extract
1 cup whole milk
⅓ cup heavy cream
¼ cup cream cheese, softened
3-6 drops purple food coloring
2 large graham crackers, broken in 1-inch pieces

Preparation:

1. In a small-sized saucepan, add the egg yolks, sugar, blueberry preserves and vanilla extract and whisk until blended thoroughly. 2. Add the milk, heavy cream, cream cheese and food coloring and whisk until blended thoroughly. 3. Place the saucepan over medium heat and cook for about 2-3 minutes, stirring continuously. 4. Remove the saucepan of milk mixture from heat and through a fine-mesh strainer, strain the mixture into an empty Ninja CREAMi pint container. 5. Place the container into an ice bath to cool. 6. After cooling, cover the container with the storage lid and freeze for 24 hours. 7. After 24 hours, remove the lid from container and arrange into the outer bowl of Ninja CREAMi. 8. Install the "Creamerizer Paddle" onto the lid of outer bowl. 9. Then rotate the lid clockwise to lock. 10. Press "Power" button to turn on the unit. 11. Then press "GELATO" button. 12. When the program is completed, with a spoon, create a 1½-inch wide hole in the center that reaches the bottom of the pint container. 13. Add the graham crackers into the hole and press "MIX-IN" button. 14. When the program is completed, turn the outer bowl and release it from the machine. 15. Transfer the gelato into serving bowls and serve immediately.

Serving Suggestions: Serve with a topping of crunchy granola.
Variation Tip: Add a few drops of lavender essential oil or a sprinkle of dried lavender for a unique and fragrant twist.
Nutritional Information per Serving:
Calories: 279 |Fat: 16g|Sat Fat: 2.1g|Carbohydrates: 28.3g|Fiber: 0.2g|Sugar: 23.7g|Protein: 6.4g

Butternut Squash and Banana Gelato

⏰ **Prep: 10 minutes** 🍲 **Cook: 3 minutes** 🍴 **Serves: 4**

Ingredients:
4 large egg yolks
1 cup heavy cream
⅓ cup granulated sugar
½ of banana, peeled and sliced
½ cup frozen butternut squash, chopped
1 (3½-ounce) box instant vanilla pudding mix
6 vanilla wafer cookies, crumbled

Preparation:
1. In a small-sized saucepan, add the egg yolks, heavy cream and sugar and whisk until blended thoroughly. 2. Place the saucepan over medium heat and cook for about 2-3 minutes, stirring continuously. 3. Remove the saucepan of egg mixture from heat and through a fine-mesh strainer, strain the mixture into an empty Ninja CREAMi pint container. 4. Place the container into an ice bath to cool. 5. After cooling, add in the banana, squash and pudding until blended thoroughly. 6. Cover the container with the storage lid and freeze for 24 hours. 7. After 24 hours, remove the lid from container and arrange into the outer bowl of Ninja CREAMi. 8. Install the "Creamerizer Paddle" onto the lid of outer bowl. 9. Then rotate the lid clockwise to lock. 10. Press "Power" button to turn on the unit. 11. Then press "GELATO" button. 12. When the program is completed, with a spoon, create a 1½-inch wide hole in the center that reaches the bottom of the pint container. 13. Add the wafer cookies into the hole and press "MIX-IN" button. 14. When the program is completed, turn the outer bowl and release it from the machine. 15. Transfer the gelato into serving bowls and serve immediately.

Serving Suggestions: Serve with a topping of fruit compote.
Variation Tip: You can use cookies of your choice.
Nutritional Information per Serving:
Calories: 296 |Fat: 17.3g|Sat Fat: 9.2g|Carbohydrates: 32.9g|Fiber: 0.8g|Sugar: 25.7g|Protein: 4.6g

Chapter 6 Gelato

Red Velvet Cream Cheese Cocoa Gelato

⏰ **Prep: 10 minutes** 🍴 **Cook: 3 minutes** 🍽 **Serves: 2**

Ingredients:

4 large egg yolks
¼ cup granulated sugar
2 tablespoons unsweetened cocoa powder
1 cup whole milk
⅓ cup heavy whipping cream
¼ cup cream cheese, softened
1 teaspoon vanilla extract
1 teaspoon red food coloring

Preparation:

1. In a small-sized saucepan, add the egg yolks, sugar and cocoa powder and whisk until blended thoroughly. 2. Add the milk, heavy cream, cream cheese, vanilla extract and food coloring and whisk until blended thoroughly. 3. Place the saucepan over medium heat and cook for about 2-3 minutes, stirring continuously. 4. Remove the saucepan of milk mixture from heat and through a fine-mesh strainer, strain the mixture into an empty Ninja CREAMi pint container. 5. Place the container into an ice bath to cool. 6. After cooling, cover the container with the storage lid and freeze for 24 hours. 7. After 24 hours, remove the lid from container and arrange into the outer bowl of Ninja CREAMi. 8. Install the "Creamerizer Paddle" onto the lid of outer bowl. 9. Then rotate the lid clockwise to lock. 10. Press "Power" button to turn on the unit. 11. Then press "GELATO" button. 12. When the program is completed, turn the outer bowl and release it from the machine. 13. Transfer the gelato into serving bowls and serve immediately.

Serving Suggestions: Serve with a topping of chocolate shaving.
Variation Tip: You can add some cinnamon and nutmeg to make a spiced red velvet gelato

Nutritional Information per Serving:
Calories: 232 |Fat: 15.6g|Sat Fat: 4.5g|Carbohydrates: 18.1g|Fiber: 0.9g|Sugar: 16g|Protein: 6.5g

Vanilla Peanut Butter Cookie Gelato

⏱ **Prep: 10 minutes**   🍴 **Cook: 6 minutes**   ❖ **Serves: 4**

Ingredients:

1 whole vanilla bean, split in half lengthwise and scraped
4 egg yolks
¾ cup heavy cream
⅓ cup whole milk
2 tablespoons granulated sugar
1 tablespoon light corn syrup
1 teaspoon vanilla extract
5 tablespoons marshmallow paste
5 peanut butter cookies, chopped

Preparation:

1. In a medium-sized saucepan, add the vanilla bean over medium-high heat, and toast for about 2-3 minutes, stirring continuously. 2. Now, adjust the heat to medium-low and whisk in the egg yolks, heavy cream, milk, sugar, corn syrup, marshmallow paste and vanilla extract. 3. Cook for about 2-3 minutes, stirring continuously. 4. Remove the pan of milk mixture from heat and through a fine-mesh strainer, strain the mixture into an empty Ninja CREAMi pint container. 5. Place the container into an ice bath to cool. 6. After cooling, cover the container with the storage lid and freeze for 24 hours. 7. After 24 hours, remove the lid from container and arrange into the outer bowl of Ninja CREAMi. 8. Install the "Creamerizer Paddle" onto the lid of outer bowl. 9. Then rotate the lid clockwise to lock. Press "Power" button to turn on the unit. 10. Then press "GELATO" button. 11. When the program is completed, with a spoon, create a 1½-inch wide hole in the center that reaches the bottom of the pint container. 12. Add the cookies into the hole and press "MIX-IN" button. 13. When the program is completed, turn the outer bowl and release it from the machine. 14. Transfer the gelato into serving bowls and serve immediately.

Serving Suggestions: Serve with a drizzling of strawberry sauce.
Variation Tip: Corn syrup can be replaced with rice syrup.
Nutritional Information per Serving:
Calories: 345 |Fat: 21g|Sat Fat: 4.3g|Carbohydrates: 31.9g|Fiber: 1.3g|Sugar: 21.1g|Protein: 6.3g

Flavorful Pumpkin Gelato

⏰ **Prep: 10 minutes**   🍲 **Cook: 3 minutes**   ❖ **Serves: 4**

Ingredients:

3 large egg yolks
⅓ cup coconut sugar
1 tablespoon corn syrup
½ cup heavy cream
1 cup whole milk
½ cup pumpkin puree
½ teaspoon ground cinnamon
½ teaspoon ground nutmeg
¾ teaspoon vanilla extract

Preparation:

1. In a small-sized saucepan, put in the egg yolks, coconut sugar and b corn syrup and whisk until blended thoroughly. 2. Put in heavy cream, whole milk, pumpkin puree and spices and whisk until blended thoroughly. 3. Place the saucepan on burner at around medium heat and cook for about 2-3 minutes, stirring continuously. 4. Take off the pan of milk mixture from burner and blend in the vanilla extract. 5. Through a fine-mesh strainer, strain the blended mixture into an empty Ninja CREAMi pint container. 6. Place the container into an ice bath to cool. 7. After cooling, cover the container with the storage lid and freeze for 24 hours. 8. After 24 hours, take off the lid from container and arrange into the outer bowl of Ninja CREAMi. 9. Install the "Creamerizer Paddle" onto the lid of outer bowl. 10. Then rotate the lid clockwise to lock. 11. Press "Power" button to turn on the unit. 12. Then press "GELATO" button. 13. When the program is completed, turn the outer bowl and release it from the machine. 14. Transfer the gelato into serving bowls and enjoy immediately.

Serving Suggestions: Serve with a topping of fresh fruit.
Variation Tip: use sugar-free pumpkin puree.
Nutritional Information per Serving:
Calories: 217 |Fat: 11.1g|Sat Fat: 5.9g|Carbohydrates: 26.2g|Fiber: 1.1g|Sugar: 21.8g|Protein: 4.7g

Carrot Gelato

⏱ **Prep: 10 minutes**   🍲 **Cook: 3 minutes**   ❖ **Serves: 4**

Ingredients:

3 large egg yolks
⅓ cup coconut sugar
1 tablespoon brown rice syrup
½ cup heavy cream
1 cup unsweetened almond milk
½ cup carrot puree
½ teaspoon ground cinnamon
¼ teaspoon ground nutmeg
¼ teaspoon ground ginger
¼ teaspoon ground cloves
¾ teaspoon vanilla extract

Preparation:

In a small-sized saucepan, add the egg yolks, coconut sugar and brown rice syrup and whisk until blended thoroughly. 2. Add the heavy cream, almond milk, carrot puree and spices and whisk until blended thoroughly. 3. Place the saucepan over medium heat and cook for about 2-3 minutes, stirring continuously. 4. Remove the pan of milk mixture from heat and stir in the vanilla extract. 5. Through a fine-mesh strainer, strain the mixture into an empty Ninja CREAMi pint container. 6. Place the container into an ice bath to cool. 7. After cooling, cover the container with the storage lid and freeze for 24 hours. 8. After cooling, cover the container with the storage lid and freeze for 24 hours. 9. After 24 hours, remove the lid from container and arrange into the outer bowl of Ninja CREAMi. 10. Install the "Creamerizer Paddle" onto the lid of outer bowl. 11. Then rotate the lid clockwise to lock. 12. Press "Power" button to turn on the unit. 13. Then press "GELATO" button. 14. When the program is completed, turn the outer bowl and release it from the machine. 15. Transfer the gelato into serving bowls and serve immediately.

Serving Suggestions: Serve with a topping of toasted nuts.
Variation Tip: You can use spices of your choice.
Nutritional Information per Serving:
Calories: 146 |Fat: 6.5g|Sat Fat: 0.9g|Carbohydrates: 22.7g|Fiber: 0.8g|Sugar: 20g|Protein: 0.8g

Sweet Potato Banana Gelato

⏰ **Prep: 10 minutes**   🍲 **Cook: 3 minutes**   🍽 **Serves: 4**

Ingredients:

4 large egg yolks
1 cup heavy cream
⅓ cup granulated sugar
½ of banana, peeled and sliced
½ cup frozen sweet potato, chopped
1 (3½-ounce) box cheesecake pudding mix
4 graham crackers, crumbled

Preparation:

1. In a small-sized saucepan, put in the egg yolks, heavy cream and sugar and whisk until blended thoroughly. 2. Place the saucepan on burner at around medium heat and cook for about 2-3 minutes, stirring continuously. 3. Take off the saucepan of egg mixture from burner and through a fine-mesh strainer, strain the blended mixture into an empty Ninja CREAMi pint container. 4. Place the container into an ice bath to cool. 5. After cooling, put in in the banana, sweet potato and pudding until blended thoroughly. 6. Cover the container with the storage lid and freeze for 24 hours. 7. After 24 hours, take off the lid from container and arrange into the outer bowl of Ninja CREAMi. 8. Install the "Creamerizer Paddle" onto the lid of outer bowl. 9. Then rotate the lid clockwise to lock. 10. Press "Power" button to turn on the unit. 11. Then press "GELATO" button. 12. When the program is completed, with a spoon, create a 1½-inch wide hole in the center that reaches the bottom of the pint container. 13. Put in crackers into the hole and press "MIX-IN" button. 14. When the program is completed, turn the outer bowl and release it from the machine. 15. Transfer the gelato into serving bowls and enjoy immediately.

Serving Suggestions: Serve with a garnishing of crushed graham crackers.
Variation Tip: Use ripe banana.
Nutritional Information per Serving:
Calories: 404 |Fat: 17.1g|Sat Fat: 8.8g|Carbohydrates: 59.3g|Fiber: 2.6g|Sugar: 24.6g|Protein: 5g

Chapter 6 Gelato |

Flavorful Cream Cheese Cacao Gelato

⏰ **Prep: 10 minutes**   🍲 **Cook: 3 minutes**   ≋ **Serves: 4**

Ingredients:

4 large egg yolks
¼ cup granulated sugar
2 tablespoons cacao powder
1 cup whole milk
⅓ cup heavy whipping cream
¼ cup cream cheese, softened
1 teaspoon vanilla extract

Preparation:

1. In a small-sized saucepan, put in the egg yolks, sugar and cacao powder and whisk until blended thoroughly. 2. Put in milk, heavy cream, cream cheese and vanilla extract and whisk until blended thoroughly. 3. Place the saucepan on burner at around medium heat and cook for about 2-3 minutes, stirring continuously. 4. Take off the saucepan of milk mixture from burner and through a fine-mesh strainer, strain the blended mixture into an empty Ninja CREAMi pint container. 5. Place the container into an ice bath to cool. 6. After cooling, cover the container with the storage lid and freeze for 24 hours. 7. After 24 hours, take off the lid from container and arrange into the outer bowl of Ninja CREAMi. 8. Install the "Creamerizer Paddle" onto the lid of outer bowl. 9. Then rotate the lid clockwise to lock. 10. Press "Power" button to turn on the unit. 11. Then press "GELATO" button. 12. When the program is completed, turn the outer bowl and release it from the machine. 13. Transfer the gelato into serving bowls and enjoy immediately.

Serving Suggestions: Serve with a garnishing of chocolate shavings.
Variation Tip: Use high-quality cacao powder.
Nutritional Information per Serving:
Calories: 232 |Fat: 15.8g|Sat Fat: 8.6g|Carbohydrates: 17.9g|Fiber: 0.8g|Sugar: 16g|Protein: 6.5g

Caramel Honey Hazelnut Gelato

⏱ **Prep: 10 minutes** 🍳 **Cook: 10 minutes** 🍽 **Serves: 4**

Ingredients:

¼ cup honey
¾ cup whole milk
½ cup hazelnut creamer
2 eggs
3 tablespoons granulated sugar
¼ cup caramels, chopped

Preparation:

1. In a medium-sized saucepan, put in honey on burner at around medium-high heat and cook for around 2-3 minutes. 2. Take off the saucepan from burner and slowly whisk in the milk and creamer. 3. Return the pan on burner at around medium-high heat and whisk in the eggs and sugar. 4. Cook for around 4-5 minutes, stirring frequently. 5. Take off the saucepan of milk mixture from burner and through a fine-mesh strainer, strain the mixture into an empty Ninja CREAMi pint container. 6. Place the container into an ice bath to cool. 7. After cooling, cover the container with the storage lid and freeze for 24 hours. 8. After 24 hours, take off the lid from container and arrange into the outer bowl of Ninja CREAMi. 9. Install the "Creamerizer Paddle" onto the lid of outer bowl. 10. Then rotate the lid clockwise to lock. 11. Press "Power" button to turn on the unit. 12. Then press "GELATO" button. 13. When the program is completed, with a spoon, create a 1½-inch wide hole in the center that reaches the bottom of the pint container. 14. Add the chopped caramels into the hole and press "MIX-IN" button. 15. When the program is completed, turn the outer bowl and release it from the machine. 16. Transfer the gelato into serving bowls and serve immediately.

Serving Suggestions: Serve with a sprinkling of sea salt.
Variation Tip: Add a splash of coffee to the gelato for a caramel latte flavor.
Nutritional Information per Serving:
Calories: 175 |Fat: 4.2g|Sat Fat: 1g|Carbohydrates: 29.6g|Fiber: 1.1g|Sugar: 26.9g|Protein: 4.7g

Conclusion

As you embark on your culinary journey with the Ninja Creami, remember that it's not just a kitchen appliance; it's a portal to a frozen wonderland. Each recipe in the book is designed to take you on a flavor-packed adventure, whether you're craving the velvety richness of ice cream or the refreshing zing of sorbet.

We've also included tips and best practices to help you become a true Ninja Creami maestro. These insights will make your frozen creations more delightful and tailored to your taste buds. Plus, our "Create Your Own" charts allow you to invent your frozen concoctions, limited only by your imagination.

So, gather your ingredients, unleash your inner chef, and let the Ninja Creami guide you on a delicious journey.

Thank you for choosing this cookbook as your guide in the delightful world of Ninja Creami.

Appendix 1 Measurement Conversion Chart

WEIGHT EQUIVALENTS

US STANDARD	METRIC (APPROXIMATE)
1 ounce	28 g
2 ounces	57 g
5 ounces	142 g
10 ounces	284 g
15 ounces	425 g
16 ounces (1 pound)	455 g
1.5 pounds	680 g
2 pounds	907 g

VOLUME EQUIVALENTS (LIQUID)

US STANDARD	US STANDARD (OUNCES)	METRIC (APPROXIMATE)
2 tablespoons	1 fl.oz	30 mL
¼ cup	2 fl.oz	60 mL
½ cup	4 fl.oz	120 mL
1 cup	8 fl.oz	240 mL
1½ cup	12 fl.oz	355 mL
2 cups or 1 pint	16 fl.oz	475 mL
4 cups or 1 quart	32 fl.oz	1 L
1 gallon	128 fl.oz	4 L

VOLUME EQUIVALENTS (DRY)

US STANDARD	METRIC (APPROXIMATE)
⅛ teaspoon	0.5 mL
¼ teaspoon	1 mL
½ teaspoon	2 mL
¾ teaspoon	4 mL
1 teaspoon	5 mL
1 tablespoon	15 mL
¼ cup	59 mL
½ cup	118 mL
¾ cup	177 mL
1 cup	235 mL
2 cups	475 mL
3 cups	700 mL
4 cups	1 L

TEMPERATURES EQUIVALENTS

FAHRENHEIT(F)	CELSIUS(C) (APPROXIMATE)
225 °F	107 °C
250 °F	120 °C
275 °F	135 °C
300 °F	150 °C
325 °F	160 °C
350 °F	180 °C
375 °F	190 °C
400 °F	205 °C
425 °F	220 °C
450 °F	235 °C
475 °F	245 °C
500 °F	260 °C

Appendix 2 Recipes Index

A

Almond Milkshake 32
Amaretto Chocolate Cookies Milkshake 32
Apple and Graham Crackers Ice Cream 48
Apricot Smoothie Bowl 25

B

Banana Coconut Smoothie Bowl 22
Banana Ice Cream 41
Banana Oreo Ice Cream 49
Banana Pineapple Rum Ice Cream 42
Banana Sorbet 16
Berries and Grapefruit Smoothie Bowl 22
Blackberry Ice Cream 44
Blueberry & Graham Cracker Ice Cream 50
Blueberry and Graham Crackers Gelato 57
Blueberry Milkshake 36
Butternut Squash and Banana Gelato 58

C

Caramel Honey Hazelnut Gelato 65
Carrot Gelato 62
Cashew Chocolate Banana Milkshake 31
Cheese Mixed Berries Gelato 56
Cheese Pecan Raspberry Ice Cream 51
Cherry Ice Cream 39
Cherry Pomegranate Sorbet 13
Chocolate Banana Milkshake 29
Chocolate Chip Cracker Ice Cream 39
Chocolate Chips Cherry Ice Cream 52
Chocolate Cookie Milkshake 34
Chocolate Peanut Gelato 54
Chocolate Sea Salt Ice Cream 52
Chocolate Spinach Ice Cream 50
Chocolate Walnut Ice cream 47
Classic Blueberry Yogurt Smoothie Bowl 26
Coconut and Berries Smoothie Bowl 20
Coconut Ice Cream 40
Coffee Ice Cream Milkshake 34

D

Delicious Caramel Ice Cream 41
Delicious Papaya Orange Smoothie Bowl 23
Dragon Fruit Smoothie Bowl 25

F

Flavorful Cream Cheese Cacao Gelato 64
Flavorful Pumpkin Gelato 61
Flavorful Sugar Cookie Vanilla Milkshake 31
Fresh Peach & Grapefruit Smoothie Bowl 24

G

Gooseberry Sorbet 18

H

Hazelnut Chocolate Milkshake 29
Healthy Apple Cherry Smoothie Bowl 27
Honey Raspberry Banana Smoothie Bowl 26

L

Lavender and Chocolate Wafer Ice Cream 48
Lemon Blueberry Sorbet 17
Lemon Oreo Ice Cream 46
Lemon Sorbet 14
Lemony Coconut Mango Sorbet 14
Lime Apple Pie Sorbet 12
Lime Mango Sorbet 15

M

Mango Smoothie Bowl 23
Maple Gelato 54
Melon & Pineapple Smoothie Bowl 24
Mint Chocolate Cookies Ice Cream 49
Mocha Ice Cream 43

O

Oat Banana Smoothie Bowl 21
Oats and Carrots Smoothie Bowl 20
Orange Sorbet 11

P

Peach Chia Seeds Smoothie Bowl 21
Peach Sorbet 12
Peanut and Grape Jelly Ice Cream 47
Peanut Butter Chips Ice Cream 51
Pear Ice Cream 44
Pear Sorbet 17
Persimmon Sorbet with Condensed Milk 13
Pineapple and Mango Sorbet 11
Pistachio Milkshake 35
Plum Sorbet 15
Pretzel Ice Cream 46
Pumpkin Brown Sugar Ice Cream 43
Pumpkin Coffee Milkshake 30

R

Raspberry Ice Cream Milkshake 36
Red Velvet Cream Cheese Cocoa Gelato 59
Refreshing Lemon Herb Sorbet 18
Refreshing Lime Avocado Ice Cream 38

S

Sea Salt Caramel Ice Cream 40
Strawberry & Dragon Fruit Banana Smoothie Bowl 27
Strawberry Shortcake Milkshake 35
Sugar Cookies Gelato 55
Sweet Apricot Sorbet 16
Sweet Coffee Gelato 55
Sweet Potato Banana Gelato 63

V

Vanilla Ice Cream Milkshake 33
Vanilla Marshmallow Oat Milkshake 30
Vanilla Oreo Milkshake 33
Vanilla Peach Ice Cream 42
Vanilla Peanut Butter Cookie Gelato 60

W

Walnut Ice Cream 38